# WELLINGTON'S
# VICTORIES

# WELLINGTON'S VICTORIES

## A GUIDE TO
## SHARPE'S ARMY
### 1797–1815

**MATTHEW MORGAN**

MICHAEL O'MARA BOOKS LIMITED

First published in Great Britain in 2004 by
Michael O'Mara Books Limited
9 Lion Yard
Tremadoc Road
London SW4 7NQ

A CIP catalogue record for this book is available from the British Library

ISBN 1-84317-093-0

1 3 5 7 9 10 8 6 4 2

Designed and typeset by Design 23

Printed and bound in Finland by WS Bookwell, Juva

# CONTENTS

# INTRODUCTION

In February 1797, twenty-seven-year-old Colonel the Hon. Arthur Wellesley, the future Duke of Wellington, went ashore at Calcutta to further his career as a soldier. As the commander of the 33rd Regiment of Foot and later as Governor of Seringapatam, it was here that Wellington distinguished himself as both a military and civilian leader, and earned himself a knighthood on his return to Britain in 1805. Ten years later, he had progressed from his role as 'sepoy general' to become the commander of the allied forces and the most famous person in Europe after Napoleon, driving the French first from Portugal and then Spain, before finally defeating Napoleon at Waterloo on 18 June 1815.

Under Wellington's command, members of the British Army were transformed from what he described as the 'scum of the earth' into an efficient, disciplined, fighting force. The army of the early nineteenth century did consist of some of the most wretched and disreputable members of British society, capable of acts of rapacious cruelty in some cases. To curb some of their more extreme behavioural excesses, Wellington duly imposed a quite severe level of discipline upon his troops; floggings were common and summary executions were also occasionally deemed necessary for restoring order in the field. Life in the British Army was hard, and Wellington believed it was necessary to be tough on his soldiers to get the best out of them. Despite lapses in discipline, therefore, the British Army did display a confidence and collective calm on the battlefield that enabled it to hold a line in the face of a seemingly relentless enemy charge. 'When we crossed the Pyrenees,' Wellington wrote, 'there never was an army in the world in better spirits, better order, or better discipline.'

Of the Duke himself, opinions varied in army circles. A lieutenant in the 30th Foot once wrote: 'No leader ever possessed so fully the confidence of his soldiers, but none did love him.' Criticized for being cold and aloof throughout his career, Wellington never inspired the adulation that Napoleon commanded from his soldiers, but neither did he crave it, as he was, above all, a servant of the Crown. Napoleon, in complete contrast, took the French crown for himself. The British commander did not embark on epic campaigns such as Napoleon's invasion of Russia, but then neither did his army experience casualties on the same scale as those endured by the French. Wellington was conspicuously careful, managing provisions and using terrain with a precision that often gave his troops the upper hand before a shot was even fired. Most importantly, Wellington was never reckless with the lives of his men, and his troops thanked him for it. He was a professional; a rational and pragmatic leader whose determination and will power made the British Army a great fighting force.

However, this book is not a guide to the life of the Duke of Wellington, nor is it in any way a summary of the Sharpe novels by Bernard Cornwell, or even a concise history of the British Army of Richard Sharpe's time. Rather, it is a miscellany: a collection of interesting, arcane, or extraordinary information about life in the many British regiments that comprised Wellington's forces between 1797 and 1815. It contains facts about the troops' uniforms, weaponry, regiments and ranks, the battles fought, the food eaten and the medical treatment the soldiers received, as well as trivia on stolen loot, the Emperor's lovers and the mystery of a horse that may or may not have been called Marengo. *Wellington's Victories* aims to give an insight into life in the army for officers and troops alike, through detail, description and anecdote.

Wellington had a dry but pithy wit and it says much of his sagacity that he was able to joke with Queen Victoria when he served as her mentor on her accession to the throne. So with quotations from both the Iron Duke's writing and from the accounts of those who knew him, the book also aims to give a sense of Wellington's thoughts on a range of subjects other than his army and his victories.

After Waterloo, the British Army would not be involved in a European war on such a scale for almost another century, and when it was, it was to be under circumstances so changed as to make the infantry little more than cannon fodder. In India, Africa and around the world, the British Army would continue to help drive the expansion of Britain's Empire so that the globe itself became a patchwork reminder of the advance of the redcoats who once patrolled it. Whatever one's view of the Empire's gradual spread, the roots of its growth lay, at least in part, in the critical victories that Wellington secured between 1797 and 1815.

## THE LIGHT-INFANTRY AND RIFLE REGIMENTS

The light infantry and the rifle regiments formed an elite within the British Army of Richard Sharpe's day (although the claim would probably have been disputed by other elite units, notably the Foot Guards, the Household Cavalry and, indeed, most if not all of the other cavalry regiments). Sharpe himself served in the 95th Rifles for some of his army career, and seems thereafter to have regarded himself as first and foremost a rifleman.

The concept of light infantry owed its inception, for the British, to the war between France and Britain in North America during the 1750s. In 1755, a small corps of 'light' troops was raised from among the British colonists, for the conspicuous uniforms and cumbersome equipment of the regular troops had proved unsuitable in action against Indians or French settlers, who knew the terrain well and used it to considerable advantage. The new corps proved remarkably effective, with the result that regular infantry regiments began to form 'Light' companies of hand-picked soldiers trained to respond to bugle calls, rather than, as previously, to drum calls. At the same time a four-battalion regiment of Foot, the 62nd (Royal American) Regiment, was raised in America from among the colonists, and a year later renumbered and renamed, becoming the 60th (Royal American) Regiment. In these events lay the seeds of both the light infantry and the rifle regiments.

The members of these units were trained as skirmishers and scouts – soldiers sent out before the line to perform a screening role to conceal from the enemy the army's most important manoeuvres, and to surprise attackers, gather intelligence, disrupt communications, neutralize the enemy's skirmishers, and slow the advance of the opposing forces. They were also trained to assemble and disperse at speed, and to act where necessary upon their own initiative, something almost unthinkable for ordinary foot soldiers in ordinary infantry units. Although trained in normal drill and manoeuvres in much the same way as other soldiers, the light infantry marched at a faster pace (140 paces to the minute to the infantry's 120), and employed more individual tactics in order to increase their effective range; firing was by single men rather than by volley, each picking his own target and shooting and reloading as quickly as he could. They too were trained to respond to bugle calls rather than shouted orders – hence the 'stringed bugle horn' badge common to light-infantry and rifle regiments.

By the time war broke out between Britain and Revolutionary France, Light companies would sometimes be ordered to operate together for particular purposes, but the raising of further specific light-infantry regiments did not begin until 1800 with the establishment of what became the 95th Rifles; in 1803 the 43rd (Monmouthshire) and 52nd (Oxfordshire) Regiments were redesignated as light infantry. Thus the original Light Brigade, raised by Major-General Sir John Moore in England in 1803, consisted of the 43rd and 52nd brigaded with the 95th (the two former would later be amalgamated to form the Oxfordshire and Buckinghamshire Light Infantry, while the 95th was renamed the Rifle Brigade in 1816). The brigade was not very formally constituted, and in 1807 the two battalions of the 95th were detached and sent to take part in the storming of Montevideo and, later, a mishandled assault on Buenos Aires. In 1809, however, the three regiments were once more together in the Light Brigade for the siege of Copenhagen, in which they served for the first time under Wellington.

On Napoleon's invasion of Spain and advance into Portugal in 1808 the brigade, under Major-General Robert Craufurd, was sent to the Peninsula, although the two battalions of the 95th were at first brigaded with the 5th Battalion, 60th (Royal American) Regiment (i.e. the 60th Rifles), before rejoining the 43rd and 52nd (both also two battalions strong) in the Light Brigade. All four regiments took part in the action at Vimiero which drove the French from Portugal. After their old commander, Moore, succeeded Wellington, the brigade took part in the advance into Spain and, when a much larger French army threatened the British force with extinction, played a distinguished part in the rearguard that covered the retreat to Corunna in January 1809, from where Moore's army was successfully evacuated by the Royal Navy (although he himself was killed in the final battle). The brigade, still under Craufurd's command (he was to die of his wounds after the capture of Ciudad Rodrigo in January 1812), returned to the Peninsula with Wellington in the summer of that year, and from then until the end of the campaign played a significant part in the succession of British victories that culminated with the French defeat at Toulouse in April 1814. In June 1815, both the 52nd and the 95th would play a dramatic and decisive part in the final defeat of Napoleon at Waterloo.

In the spring of 1810, Wellington reformed the Light Brigade into the Light Division by adding two battalions of Portuguese light infantry (*cacadores*; literally, hunters), part of his general move to reorganize his army into divisions. Unquestionably the Light Brigade and its successor, the Light Division, were the elite of the British and allied forces in the Peninsula.

In time, other regiments were redesignated as light infantry: in 1808 the 68th Foot and the 85th, in 1809 the 51st and the 71st, and in 1815 the 90th (later to become, respectively, the Durham Light Infantry, the 2nd Battalion, King's Shropshire LI, the King's Own Yorkshire LI, the Highland Light Infantry, and the Cameronians [Scottish Rifles]).

The French Army of the Napoleonic era had its own light infantry in the shape of *Voltigeurs* (literally, acrobats), so called because of their agility, and were recruited for their smallness of stature and speed of movement. The Prussian and Austrian equivalent of a light infantryman or rifleman was, like his Portuguese counterpart, called a *Jäger*, literally, hunter.

## THE RIFLEMEN

The adoption of rifled weapons changed the battlefield for ever, but in the late eighteenth and early nineteenth centuries they were a rarity, their issue confined to a few specialist corps. By far the majority of European infantry regiments were armed with smoothbore muskets, whose effective accuracy was little more than 40 yards. For this reason, infantry in battle tended to manoeuvre and fight in relatively large units – companies and sometimes whole battalions – in order to concentrate their firepower by delivering well-drilled volleys of fire at a single target. Given sufficient powder and shot, a well-handled and well-disciplined infantry battalion, especially when formed into a square, could break or drive off even the most determined assault by infantry advancing in line or by charging cavalry; only accurate artillery fire could disperse such a formation (and the cannon of the day were smoothbore weapons as well, and therefore increasingly inaccurate at lengthening ranges, while gun batteries were also vulnerable to being overrun by cavalry or even infantry at shorter ranges). The coming of the rifle allowed a change in tactics: now much smaller units of men, employing light-infantry methods, could strike at enemy targets at distances well beyond effective musket range. Riflemen therefore provided harassing fire from a distance at which their musket-armed adversaries could not reply, and then melted away as the enemy came within musket range.

The first true rifle unit in the British Army was the 5th Battalion of the 60th (Royal American) Regiment, which was raised in 1797. Under its forward-thinking commander, Baron Francis de Rottenberg (whose theories about light infantry and riflemen heavily influenced Moore), its men were trained in the light-infantry tactics of its parent regiment, but armed with rifles rather than muskets, and, among other differences of equipment and clothing, were dressed in dark green uniforms rather than the scarlet of most of the Line infantry. To the 60th, therefore, belongs the honour of being the first true British rifle regiment, and in the Peninsular campaign Wellington ordered that the 5th Battalion should provide companies of riflemen to each of his other infantry divisions.

In 1800, the spirit of both light infantry and the Rifles was carried forward with the establishment of the 'Experimental Corps of Riflemen', which was formed from 443 volunteers of all ranks from fifteen Line regiments. An elite force issued with the specialist Baker rifle, it was renamed the Rifle Corps before becoming, in 1802, the 95th or Rifle Regiment (later the 95th Rifles). Like the 60th, its members took advantage of the Baker rifle's greater reach and accuracy by hitting specific targets at long range, using light-infantry tactics instead of relying on the massed attacks that characterized other British infantry armed with muskets.

In 1816, the 95th was taken out of the numbered Line regiments and renamed the Rifle Brigade (the Derbyshire Regiment, later the 2nd Battalion, the Sherwood Foresters, taking over the designation 95th Foot). Richard Sharpe joined the 2nd Battalion of the 95th Rifles in July 1805. From then on, he regarded himself as a rifleman, even though he only spent three and a half years in the battalion; in *Sharpe's Revenge*, for instance, which is mainly set after Napoleon's defeat in 1814, and by which time Sharpe is serving as a staff officer, he and his companions travel on a private mission across France wearing the faded green tunics of their Rifle regiments.

Issued with black leather belts (the ordinary infantry wore white belts, which had to be kept white with pipeclay, a tedious business), dark green jackets (a colour known as 'rifle green') and trousers and a 'stovetop' shako surmounted by a dark green cockade, riflemen were easily distinguished from the average British soldier. In addition, they carried a long 'sword' bayonet, necessary because the Baker rifle was shorter than the Brown Bess musket, and to this day Rifle regiments still use the command 'Fix swords' rather than 'Fix bayonets'. They were, from the start, an elite: among riflemen, discipline was to be valued alongside trust and respect for fellow soldiers. A recruiting poster for the 95th from 1808 read: 'On Service, your Post is always the Post of Honour, and your Quarters the best in the Army; for you have the first of every thing; and at Home you are sure of Respect – because a BRITISH RIFLEMAN always makes himself Respectable' – one line also trumpeted: 'NO WHITE BELTS NO PIPE CLAY'. Since riflemen were generally deployed as individuals or in small groups, they carried no colours, and in action reacted to whistle blasts and bugle calls rather than the beating of drums. The 95th were nicknamed 'The Sweeps' for their dark green uniforms and 'The Grasshoppers' for their agile skirmishing. At least one battalion of the 95th was present at every major battle in the Peninsula except Albuera, and throughout the campaign they acted as both a forward force when in advance and as a covering force when in retreat. Hence the regiment's proud boast, 'First in the field and last out of it'; indeed, Wellington's standing orders insisted that the 60th and the 95th should always form the vanguard when his army was on the move.

# DIVISIONS

Although the dividing up of the army into brigades had been attempted previously, Wellington was the first man to institute a fixed divisional system. In the Peninsula he mixed battalions of raw recruits and experienced veterans together into divisions of between two and four infantry brigades. A division came under the command of a lieutenant-general; it acted as a miniature army and greatly strengthened British forces.

A rifle company (principally from the 60th Regiment's 5th Battalion) was assigned to each division. Initially there was not enough artillery available to every division for permanent use, but this changed over time. A crucial innovation in the Peninsula was the inclusion of a five-battalion Portuguese brigade combined with two British brigades, which became the Anglo–Portuguese divisions; they were approximately 5,800 strong, with around 3,500 British and 2,300 Portuguese soldiers in each. The Light Division was formed in the spring of 1810 by adding two Portuguese *Cacadores* battalions to Robert Craufurd's Light Brigade. Unlike the French, Wellington only rarely grouped two or more divisions together as a corps under a senior general, which was something that Napoleon instituted as a permanent feature.

## Summary of specific divisions

1ST DIVISION: Comprising 7,000 soldiers, which made it the army's largest division, it contained Guards regiments and as a result was nicknamed 'The Gentlemen's Sons'.

2ND DIVISION: This division was positioned on the right flank of the army, and was known as 'The Observing Division'.

3RD DIVISION: Renowned for being tough fighters both on and away from the battlefield and nicknamed 'The Fighting Division', most recruits were drawn from Irish peasant stock.

4TH DIVISION: This division regularly provided valuable support to the 2nd Division, and was hence known as 'The Supporting Division'; after the siege of Albuera, however, it was renamed 'The Enthusiastics'.

5TH DIVISION: Involved in widespread road-building in 1810, this division earned the nickname 'The Pioneers'.

6TH DIVISION: Known particularly for its extensive marching and counter-marching without engaging the enemy before Salamanca in 1812, it was named 'The Marching Division'.

7TH DIVISION: Because it contained four foreign battalions and only two British, and included the Brunswickers and Chasseurs Britanniques whose desertion levels were high, it was referred to as 'The Mongrels'.

LIGHT DIVISION: Containing about 4,000 soldiers, this division became the army's elite formation, taking on a screening role to shield the main army and harass the enemy; it called itself '*The* Division'.

## BRIGADES

Below the divisions in the hierarchy of military formations came the brigades, each normally comprising a tactical grouping of two or three (or occasionally four) infantry battalions or two cavalry regiments. When forming part of a division, a brigade had no internal support, but when operating independently, it might contain a proportionate number of supporting units, such as artillery, cavalry, engineers, and supply and transport services.

There was no standard organization for infantry brigades in the Peninsula until 1809, when Wellington began forming them into divisions. Subsequently, during the Waterloo campaign of 1815, his policy was to have two or three brigades in each division and three to five battalions in each brigade. In the Peninsula in 1810, however, Lieutenant-General Sir Rowland Hill's 2nd Division comprised three British brigades and Hamilton's Portuguese Division, which contained two brigades, whereas Major-General Thomas Picton's 3rd Division consisted of two British and one Portuguese brigade. Nor was the rank of brigade commanders standardized. On occasion a brigade might be commanded by the senior of the battalion commanders (that is, a lieutenant-colonel or, sometimes, colonel), while on others it might be commanded by a brigadier-general or indeed by a major-general.

At that date, brigades were known by the names of the brigade commanders; thus De Grey's Brigade of heavy cavalry consisted of the 3rd Dragoon Guards and the 4th Dragoons, under Brigadier-General the Hon. George de Grey, while Stopford's Brigade of Lieutenant-General Sir Brent Spencer's 1st Division comprised the 1st Battalion, 2nd (Coldstream) Guards and 1st Battalion, 3rd (Scots) Guards under Major-General Kenneth Stopford.

Arguably the best known of Wellington's infantry brigades, the 6th or 'Light' Brigade, commanded by the legendary Major-General Robert 'Black Bob' Craufurd (until his death in 1812), also fired the first shots of the Peninsular War at a Portuguese village called Obidos in 1808. The Light Brigade had been specifically trained to carry out tactical reconnaissance and to protect an army when both advancing or withdrawing, duties that had previously been carried out by light cavalry, although the latter still fulfilled its reconnaissance role.

Besides the infantry, Wellington's army in the Peninsula had by 1810 five cavalry brigades, four British and one Portuguese, each of the former made up of two cavalry regiments (roughly equivalent to an infantry battalion). The army was further supported by artillery, which was in turn sub-divided into horse and field artillery (that is, batteries from the Royal Horse Artillery and the Royal Artillery), Portuguese artillery and the artillery of the King's German Legion.

## REGIMENTS

It could perhaps be argued that there is no such thing as a 'British Army', but rather a collection of corps and regiments. Certainly, in being based, almost from the first, on a regimental system, in which soldiers often remained (and indeed remain) with the same unit throughout their service, the British Army, largely unlike its European and, later, American, counterparts, did not follow convention. Such an arrangement helped foster highly effective combat forces, shaped as they were by bonds of friendship, loyalty, pride and a commitment to their regiment's tradition. Indeed, the regimental system of the British Army was – and still is – an unusual hotchpotch of tradition, rank, loyalty and pride, which through the centuries has given rise to a military history as distinguished and unique as the regiments themselves.

As a unit of martial force, the regiment evolved from within the infantry, and was characterized by being commanded by a colonel who originally possessed, under a warrant from the Crown, overall responsibility for arming, clothing, disciplining, training and paying the regiment. In the later part of the seventeenth and early eighteenth centuries the majority of cavalry and infantry regiments were known by their colonels' names. The infantry, or regiments of Foot, formed the heart of the British Army; also known also as 'infantry of the Line', or 'Line regiments', the infantry were the mainstay of battle, withstanding the brunt of the enemy's attack, and striving to advance to take his territory.

From 1751, the regiments were numbered in order of seniority, which depended upon the date at which they had been formed. The 1st Regiment of Foot (later the Royal Scots, nicknamed 'Pontius Pilate's Bodyguards') was established in 1625 as John Hepburn's Regiment, and in 1751 it was consequently given the numeral that established it as the oldest regiment of Line infantry. By the end of the Napoleonic Wars in 1815, there were over one hundred infantry regiments, as well as the unnumbered Rifle Brigade (though formerly it existed as the 95th Regiment of Foot). After 1782, regiments were also allocated a territorial title which in some cases was a formality, but it is by this designation that some of the more famous regiments are still remembered, such as the Connaught Rangers, the old 88th and 94th Foot, disbanded in 1922. The names persist even today, after so many amalgamations and disbandments have seen a number of regimental names disappear for ever.

A regiment was both an administrative and a fighting unit, usually comprising one or more battalions each formed of ten 'companies'. By the latter part of the seventeenth century, eight of the ten companies were formed of ordinary soldiers, the other two being a company of grenadiers and one of light infantry (Grenadier and Light Companies respectively). Historically, and as their name suggests, grenadiers were equipped with grenades and were often the finest, strongest and tallest men, marching in the vanguard of the column and delivering the regiment's show of force. The light infantry, less heavily armed and equipped than their counterparts in the other companies, were skirmishers, fast and mobile, designed to harass the enemy and hamper their advance. See pages 10-12 for further information on the light infantry.

A regiment's colours (or guidons and standards for cavalry regiments) were at the heart of its identity, figuratively and literally. In battle, the flag bearing the regiment's badge was always situated in the middle of the formation, providing a point on which the soldiers could fix to ensure they fought and moved together. The colours were an obvious target for the enemy, however, as capturing them not only ensured military glory, but contributed to the disarray of the regiment and weakened its fighting ability. The life expectancy of the ensign (the junior officer who usually carried the colour) was brutally short, as was that of any man who hoisted the colour aloft if the ensign fell.

This remarkable loyalty to the regiment was perhaps, and perhaps still is, its defining characteristic; there was an intense pride in the unit's military achievements and in the unique 'personality' of the regiment, which was frequently reflected in its uniform, nickname and motto. The metal cap badges and insignia worn on the uniforms often spoke of a trait or accolade symbolic to that regiment – the stringed bugle of the light infantry and the rifle regiments being a good example – and the use of metal signified the permanence of the regiment as a unit, in contrast to the cloth badges that would identify more transient formations. The spirit of comradeship fostered by such 'tribal' traditions is evident throughout Cornwell's fiction, and in Sharpe's participation in regimental life can be seen something of just how vital these fighting groups were to the British Army.

## Regiments in which Sharpe served

33rd Regiment of Foot (later the Duke of Wellington's Regiment)
74th Regiment of Foot (Highland) (later the 2nd Battalion, the Highland Light Infantry)
95th Regiment (95th Rifle Regiment, later the Rifle Brigade)
South Essex (fictional)

## BATTALIONS

Unlike the French or most European armies, a British infantry regiment was not a tactical formation. Instead it raised between one and four battalions, a battalion being the regiment's tactical unit on the battlefield. With at least two battalions, a regiment could keep one battalion at home and send another into the field to replace those who had been killed, injured or who had fallen ill. In 1809 there were 179 Line battalions, of which only 28 were stationed in the Peninsula. Seventy remained at home, twenty-seven were based in the West Indies, twenty-three in the East Indies, and fourteen in Sicily and Malta, with others in Canada, the Cape Colony, New South Wales, Gibraltar and Madeira. A regiment was referred to by its number and if it contained more than one battalion, that number preceded the regimental number: for example, the 1/44th was the 1st Battalion of the 44th Regiment of Foot.

In 1809 the average battalion strength of the infantry was 980 officers and men, but units on active service were often smaller in size. In the Peninsular War many battalions struggled to remain viable fighting forces. By 1811 there were forty-six battalions on the Peninsula. Only nine of these had more than 700 men on active service and the rest had an average of 550; one had only 263 soldiers. Sometimes a regiment's second battalion was called into service but it would usually be reduced in strength, having already contributed drafts of men to the first. A battalion came under the command of a lieutenant-colonel, along with two majors, ten captains and thirty subalterns plus an adjutant, paymaster, quartermaster and surgeon (sometimes with an assistant).

## COMPANIES

Each battalion incorporated ten companies of up to a hundred men. Controlled through signals by drum and trumpet, the companies were small enough to maintain a sense of unity and common purpose, but large enough to threaten an enemy formation. A battalion was most exposed on its flanks, so it needed to have its most experienced men to protect them there. In each of these flanking companies, the sergeants carried muskets instead of pikes, and their officers carried curved sabres. The soldiers wore lace-embellished wings on their shoulders and the officers wore a more elaborate version in gold braid. The right-flank company had formerly been issued with grenades and so were called the 'Grenadiers'. They were generally taller than the rest of the battalion and maintained an air of superiority. The left-flank company, known as the 'Light company', contained many of the battalion's best shots.

## Relative ranks in the British and Indian Armies

| British | Indian equivalent |
| --- | --- |
| Captain | Subadar |
| Lieutenant | Jemadar |
| Sergeant-Major | Havildar-Major |
| Sergeant | Havildar |
| Corporal Naik | Private Sepoy |

## Relative ranks in the British and French Armies

| British | French equivalent |
| --- | --- |
| Field Marshal | *Maréchal* |
| General | *Général d'Armée* |
| Lieutenant-General | *Général de Corps d'Armée* |
| Major-General | *Général de Division* |
| Brigadier-General | *Général de Brigade* |
| Colonel | *Colonel* |
| Lieutenant-Colonel | *Lieutenant-Colonel* |
| Major | *Chef de Bataillon* |
| Captain | *Capitaine* |
| Lieutenant | *Lieutenant* |
| 2nd Lieutenant | *Sous-Lieutenant* |
| Regimental Sergeant-Major, Warrant Officer | *Adjutant-Chef, Adjutant Sous-Officier* |
| Sergeant | *Sergent* |
| Corporal | *Caporal* |
| Private | *Soldat* |

## ARMY RECRUITMENT

The British Army, which reached its peak of 233,852 officers and men in 1815, was in constant need of new recruits. Reasons for joining up included:

> unemployment
> destitution
> boredom with home life
> trouble with the law
> overbearing parents
> desire to cheat the army out of the King's shilling

Regulations in 1802 stated:
'In the Infantry, Men enlisted ... are not to be taken above Twenty-five years of Age, nor less than Five Feet Six inch high; but growing Lads from Seventeen to Nineteen Years of Age, may be taken as low as Five Feet Five [Four] Inches... The Lads and Boys are to be enlisted as Privates, without any Promise or Expectation being held out to them that they are to be of the Band, or put on Drummer's Pay.'

The army employed a large number of 'recruiting parties' who would go out in the country and actively encourage able-bodied men to sign up. A recruiting sergeant would set up in a town with a drummer, both working on commission, and inspire the local men to join. An 1814 poster for the 7th Light Dragoons is typical of the rousing tone:

THE OLD SAUCY SEVENTH,
Or Queen's Own Regt. Of Lt. Dragoons.
COMMANDED BY THAT GALLANT AND
WELL KNOWN HERO,
Lieut. General HENRY LORD PAGET.
YOUNG fellows whose hearts beat high to tread the paths of
Glory, could not have a better opportunity than now offers.
Come forward then, and Enrol yourselves in a Regiment that
stands unrivalled, and where the kind treatment the Men ever

experienced is well known throughout the whole Kingdom.
*Each young Hero on being approved, will receive the largest*
*Bounty allowed by Government.*
*A few smart Young Lads will be taken by Sixteen Years of Age,*
*5 Feet 2 Inches, but they must be active, and well limbed.*
*Apply to SERJEANT HOOPER...*

N.B. This Regiment is mounted on Blood Horses, and
being lately returned from SPAIN, and the Horses Young,
the Men will not be allowed to HUNT during the next
Season, more than once a week.

The recruiting sergeant might talk of a bounty of over two
month's wages, the 'seduction factor' of a man in uniform, or
concessions limiting the time of service from the usual twenty-
five years to seven. If neither the drums of war nor the recruiting
sergeant's bribes convinced the potential recruit, then they
would resort to getting him drunk to achieve their aims. It was
often in a smoky tavern, after consuming far too much rum, that
a young man signed up for life. A significant minority also came
through the 'King's hard bargains': pickpockets, thieves and
other rogues forced to choose between the army or jail.
Consequently, almost every battalion had its share of drunkards,
thieves and malcontents.

Once given the bounty, or having taken 'the King's shilling', the
would-be soldier was given a perfunctory medical examination
(failed by roughly a third of new recruits) before being attested
before a magistrate. Finally, he took two oaths: the Oath of
Fidelity to the King and Army, and the Oath of Allegiance,
which covered the right of the Crown to transfer him to the East
India Company's forces if he was needed there.

From his initial bounty, the recruit had to pay for part of his
uniform and other miscellaneous expenses. He could also look
forward to being welcomed by his new regiment – as long as he
had the bounty in his pocket and was willing to buy everyone a

drink. Although wartime governments resorted to the large-scale recruitment of foreigners, they also looked for new ways to recruit from home in addition to the recruiting party. After the renewal of war with France in 1803, fears grew that Britain faced an increased risk from invasion, and so the government took steps to improve defence and boost numbers in the county militia regiments, as well as creating new volunteer forces to help protect the country. Thus, as a result of passing two Acts in July 1803 'to enable His Majesty more effectually to raise and assemble . . . an additional Military Force, for the better Defence and Security of the United Kingdom, and for the more vigorous Prosecution of the War', the Army of Reserve was established. It was a far from popular means of recruiting able-bodied men (being a system not unlike conscription), but while certain numbers had to be raised from volunteers or by ballot from each county, some men were also exempt from duty, including those at university, teachers or clergymen, seamen or justices of the peace.

In order to become an officer, a man could either purchase a commission in a regiment or he could be granted a commission by presenting a letter of recommendation from an appropriate person. As a result, there were very few officers from working-class backgrounds, except for a handful of men promoted from the ranks for exceptional qualities or service. About two-thirds of commissions in the seventeenth and eighteenth centuries were obtained by purchase; a commission in a line regiment would sometimes cost over a thousand pounds. Usually, a young man would buy a position as an ensign in the infantry or a cornet in the cavalry, and go on to buy successive promotions as other vacancies appeared. An officer selling his commission would normally offer it first to the most senior officer below him, which would set off a chain reaction of buying and selling throughout the regiment. Theoretically, commissions were bought from and sold back to the government, although the regimental agent usually handled the transaction. The system of purchasing commissions was designed to avoid the need to provide officers with pensions on their retirement. In effect, they carried their pensions with them, so that when they 'sold out' they had a tidy sum of money to sustain them in later life. Those officers intending to embark upon the longest and most prosperous careers strove to obtain commissions in senior regiments. Commissions were also gained through patronage, as a reward for distinguished service.

In times of war, when the high casualties among officers ensured that the demand for them outstripped supply, as many as four-fifths of commissions were obtained without purchase. It was in such circumstances that Richard Sharpe was able to rise through the ranks. However, the position of non-commissioned officers (NCOs) was invariably thankless, for they were treated with disdain by 'gentleman' officers, and with distrust by the troops below them.

## THE QUARTERMASTER

In *Sharpe's Rifles*, Sharpe is appointed quartermaster, which was, in effect, the supply staff officer to the colonel, a post often given to someone who had risen through the ranks. The post of quartermaster was an administrative one of great importance but he was not regarded as a combatant officer. According to *The Regimental Companion* (1804), 'The quartermaster is not to do any duty other than quartermaster while the regiment is on actual service. His duty is, to take care of the ammunition and stores of the regiment; to attend to all deliveries of coals, forage etc. and to prevent frauds from being committed against the public service.' Quartermasters always have the letters (QM) written after their rank, thus: Captain (QM) followed by the officer's name.

## FOREIGN CORPS

All major armies recruited foreign troops. In 1804, foreign corps formed 11 per cent of the British Army and in 1813 they constituted more than 20 per cent. At Waterloo, Wellington commanded more German-speaking troops than English-speaking.

**The King's German Legion:** The KGL was the largest and best foreign corps in British service, with roots in the Hanoverian army, which was raised in response to the French invasion of Hanover in 1803. The legion contained line and light infantry, hussars, dragoons and artillery, peaking in size at over 14,000 men in June 1812. The cavalry were skilled horsemen, and Captain Cavalié Mercer of the Royal Horse Artillery commented that 'affection for, and care of, his horse, is the trait, *par excellence*, which distinguishes the German dragoon from the English. The former would sell everything to feed his horse; the latter would sell his horse for spirits, or the means of obtaining them.' Respected and well-liked, the KGL fought with distinction in the Peninsular War and at Waterloo and, when disbanded, many of its former soldiers went on to serve in the Hanoverian or British armies.

**The Brunswick-Oels Corps:** This corps was raised in 1809 by the Duke of Brunswick, whose father had been killed commanding the Prussian forces against Napoleon. After a period with the Austrian army, it marched across Europe and was evacuated by the Royal Navy. Members of the Brunswick-Oels Corps were known as the Black Brunswickers (because of the colour of their uniforms), as well as the 'Death or Glory Men' (from their skull-and-crossbones badge). Initially they were good fighters, but when the Prussian officers and German rank-and-file volunteers dried up, they had to resort to recruiting from British prisoner-of-war camps, resulting in a motley assortment of German, Polish, Swiss, Danish, Dutch and Croatian turncoats, many of whom deserted. Consequently, the corps became poorly regarded among other British troops. The Duke of Brunswick himself was killed at Quatre Bras in June 1815.

**The Chasseurs Britanniques**: Perhaps the strangest – and most unreliable – foreign corps that served in the British Army, the Chasseurs Britanniques were the only nominally French troops to serve with Wellington in the Peninsular War. The corps was known for an appalling rate of desertion, to which it lost 224 men during 1813 alone.

Other foreign troops to come under British command during the Napoleonic period included the Calabrian Free Corps, the Ceylon Light Dragoons, the Piedmontese Legion, the Greek Light Infantry, the Nassauers and the Hanoverians.

## THE IRISH QUESTION

Nicknamed 'Patlanders', accused of being dirty and verminous, reviled as cheap labour in peacetime and forever the butt of jokes among fellow soldiers, the Irish nevertheless made up a significant proportion of the British Army, including 42 per cent of the Royal Artillery. In combat, they had few peers, as when the 88th (Connaught Rangers) were instrumental in taking Ciudad Rodrigo in January 1812. Lieutenant William Grattan regarded the Irish soldier with some esteem: 'He can live on as little nourishment as a Frenchman; give him a pipe of tobacco and he will march for two days without food and without *grumbling*; give him, in addition, a little spirits and a biscuit, and he will work for a week.' Also known for their humour, the Irish occupied an ambivalent position in the British Army through serving the army of an occupying power, until the Act of Union brought the countries together in 1801, three years after the Great Rebellion of 1798 (which received French support) had thrown much of Ireland into turmoil, and thoroughly alarmed Britain. Many Irish soldiers balanced an instinctive nationalism with a practical professionalism for the army that they served, singing rebel songs as they marched to the British drums.

## GUERRILLAS

In the Peninsular campaign, Wellington often bemoaned his Spanish allies, especially those such as the obstinate Don Gregorio Garcia de la Cuesta, but he maintained a high regard for the guerrillas who proved vital in harassing the French forces and intercepting communications between Spain and France. The guerrillas invariably had moustaches, heavy belts and bands of ammunition strung around their waists and across their shoulders, which were concealed beneath heavy cloaks. They were a fiery mixture of fugitives from the Spanish army, criminals, smugglers, escaped prisoners of war, patriots, monks and priests. Cura Merino, the most famous such priest, specialized in castrating French officers. Some were bandits first and patriots second who terrorized large areas of the countryside, but all hated the French with a passion and they soon earned a reputation for bravery and ruthlessness.

A Spanish guerrilla leader called Moreno (whom Sharpe would actually meet in *Sharpe's Gold*) was said to have killed seven French soldiers with a single shot from his blunderbuss, the recoil of which dislocated his shoulder. When presenting some captured silver to the people of his hometown, the Spaniard decorated one such piece with a selection of French ears. The French were brutal in their turn, which spurred the Spanish on to further acts of cruelty that included skinning or boiling them alive and crucifying them upside down. Francisco Goya's horrific series of etchings, 'The Disasters of War', depicted the effects of the Peninsular War upon the ordinary people of Spain.

## SPANISH RECRUITS

As late as 1811, Wellington had been against recruiting Spanish troops into the army. Sceptical of their loyalty and their ability, he was, nonetheless, desperately short of reinforcements from either Portugal or Britain, and had to find an alternative supply. His army had suffered heavily at Ciudad Rodrigo and Badajoz in 1812, and with war in the United States looming and renewed fighting in other British colonies, troops were being diverted elsewhere.

In May 1812 an agreement was duly reached to enlist 5,000 Spanish into the British ranks. Recruitment proved difficult at first, since many of the young men who remained in the villages were either unfit or unwilling, but by the end of the year regiments that had recruited successfully included the 95th Rifles, who took forty-six Spaniards into their 1st Battalion and nine into their 3rd Battalion. Many Spanish recruits were promoted to corporal and Sir Harry Smith, 1st Battalion, 95th Rifles, offered due praise: 'We had also ten men a Company in our British Regiments, Spaniards, many of them the most daring of sharpshooters in our corps, who nobly regained the distinction attached to the name of Spanish infantry of Charles V's time. I never saw better, more orderly, perfectly sober soldiers in my life . . .'

The only negative aspect of the Spanish recruits seemed to be their propensity for murdering and mutilating wounded Frenchmen. When the Peninsular War came to an end, however, the Spaniards were discharged from the British Army; a sad event for British soldier and Spaniard alike.

## RATES OF PAY

Pay varied greatly between ranks and between arms of service. When a soldier first joined the army, he would be offered a bounty to join, its size fluctuating with the scale of demand. Once in the army, the soldier would discover that much of the money they had expected to receive would have to be spent on essentials, such as clothes. Compared to French or Prussian conscripts, the average British soldier did reasonably well, but compared to almost any of their countrymen his pay was poor. When stationed in places such as India, money went further, but those who joined up to make their fortune from foreign gold soon found that the spoils of war were not for everyone. It was an offence to keep items without handing them over to the prize agent, but the temptation was obviously to slip the item into one's coat and hope nobody noticed.

### British Army – daily rate of pay in 1800

|  | CAVALRY | INFANTRY | MILITIA |
|---|---|---|---|
| Colonel | 32s 10d | 22s 6d | 22s |
| Major | 23s | 14s 1d | 14s 1d |
| Captain | 14s 7d | 9s 5d | 9s 5d |
| Lieutenant | 9s | 4s 8d | 4s 8d |
| Ensign |  | 3s 8d | 3s 8d |
| Cornet | 8s |  | 3s 8d |
| Paymaster | 15s | 15s | 15s |
| Quartermaster |  | 4s 8d | 4s 8d |
| Surgeon | 11s 4d | 9s 5d | 9s 5d |
| Asst Surgeon | 5s | 5s | 5s |
| Sergeant | 2s 11d | 1s 7d | 1s 7d |
| Corporal | 2s 5d | 1s 3d | 1s 3d |
| Trumpeter | 2s 4d |  |  |
| Fifer/drummer |  | 1s 2d |  |
| Private | 2s | 1s | 1s |

## Daily rate of pay for British officers in 1815

|  | CAVALRY | INFANTRY |
|---|---|---|
| Colonel | 32s 10d | 22s 6d |
| Major | 23s | 17s |
| Captain | 14s 7d | 10s 6d |
| Lieutenant | 9s | 6s 6d |
| Ensign |  | 5s 3d |
| Cornet | 5s 3d |  |
| Paymaster | 15s | 15s |
| Quartermaster |  | 8s |
| Surgeon | 11s 4d | 11s 4d |

s = shillings; d = pence

In India the differences between pay awarded to Indian and British troops was enormous, but the sepoys still lived comparatively well compared to their countrymen.

|  | INDIAN | BRITISH |
|---|---|---|
| Private | 6 rupees | 30 shillings (15 rupees) |
| Corporal | 8 rupees | 40 shillings (20 rupees) |
| Sergeant | 10 rupees | 55 shillings (28 rupees) |
| Officers | 16–60 rupees | 120 shillings (60 rupees) |

# INFANTRY WEAPONS

## Muskets

Muzzle-loading, smoothbore flintlock muskets were the main weapon of foot soldiers. They fired a spherical ball of varying sizes according to the calibre of the weapon. The regular British musket, introduced in 1768, was officially called the Short Land Musket (New Pattern) and was nicknamed 'Brown Bess', possibly from Dutch *bus*, meaning gun (as in blunderbuss, an alteration of Dutch *donderbus*, 'thunder gun'), and perhaps from the weapon's brown woodwork or because the barrel was treated with a chemical process that made it brown in colour. The Prussian musket was the Prussian Potsdam and the regular French musket was the Charleville, named after the gunworks at which they were produced. Lasting from eight to ten years, however, Brown Bess was generally considered the best musket in Europe. The average British ball weighed about an ounce and at close range could smash bones and cause massive bleeding. Soldiers carried approximately sixty cartridges that were already made up with gunpowder and ball or shot wrapped in greased paper, in a flapped leather pouch with a slotted wooden interior. The composition of gunpowder varied among the various armies but British gunpowder was usually made up from quantities of charcoal, saltpetre and sulphur.

In the process of loading the musket, the soldier bit the end off the paper cartridge, often retaining the bullet or shot in his mouth; a practice that would apparently cause a terrible thirst and blackened lips. The soldier then pulled back the flint jaws of the cock a single notch to the half-cock position, before pushing the 'frizzen' (hammer) towards the muzzle, which opened the priming pan. Next he dribbled a small quantity of powder into the pan and clicked the frizzen back down to cover the powder. Then the musket butt was grounded and the rest of the powder was emptied down the barrel before the ball was dropped down on top. The next step involved the ramrod, which the soldier took from beneath the musket's barrel, and used to force the empty paper cartridge down the barrel. Thus the combination of paper, ball and powder was made firm and compact at the bottom of the barrel. The ramrod was put back in its slot under the barrel, and the soldier put the musket in a horizontal position. In the final stage, the trigger was primed and ready for use after the cock was drawn back to the full-cock position. At this point the musket was raised and then fired. As the cock flew downwards the flint struck the steel to produce sparks, and the steel moved forward, thus exposing the powder-filled flash-pan to the sparks. There was a brief pause while the powder in the pan ignited, and then the main charge fired with a roar much like a modern shotgun, projecting the musket ball towards its intended target.

With so many men packed closely together, individuals were in danger both from shot and scorching from the sparks that flew out of the muskets, which could set fire to hair or clothes. Misfires were common, and the build-up of residue from the powder that collected in the barrels had to be cleaned using wire brushes that the soldiers carried with them. However in wet or windy weather the priming powder might fail to ignite. Sometimes, even if it did catch light, there would only be 'a flash in the pan', which was not enough to set off the main charge. Occasionally, soldiers forgot to remove the ramrod from the barrel and pulled the trigger when it was still inside. In the chaos of battle it was common for a man to believe that his musket had fired, when in fact it hadn't, so he would start reloading without realizing he still had a quantity of powder and a shot within the barrel. A subsequent ignition might not fire properly, and end up wasting valuable seconds in battle; worse still, there was also the danger it could blow the weapon to pieces.

On average it took at least thirty seconds to load a musket, although this could vary depending on the skill of each soldier. There were short cuts that could be taken such as skipping the ramming procedure, and simply coaxing the ball on to the powder by rapping the musket butt sharply against the ground.

A well-rammed weapon could also deliver a heavy kick, which was another reason to cut out the ramming stage, or at least not use so much power to pack it in. However, this not only reduced the force of the ball when it emerged from the muzzle, but sometimes caused it to fall out of the barrel, especially if the firer was aiming downwards. The Brown Bess also lacked precision – a marksman had a chance of hitting a man at eighty yards, but beyond this range an accurate shot was unlikely. However, despite all its shortcomings, the Brown Bess dictated warfare for a century, and remained in active use until 1853.

## Rifles

The rifle had almost three times the range of a musket, and a shot fired at up to 200 yards by a trained man would be certain to hit and kill the target. In a rifle, the inside of the barrel was scored in a way to give the ball spin and increase the accuracy of the shot. The weapon was in short supply, and was generally only issued to the best marksmen or regiments in the army, such as the 95th (later the Rifle Brigade), who were capable of causing the most damage. The early 'rifles' were still essentially muskets and so were also muzzle loaded.

The 'Baker' was the most popular rifle of the period, designed for the Experimental Corps of Riflemen by a Whitechapel manufacturer called Ezekiel Baker. Its precision owed much to the seven grooves which made a quarter turn down the barrel. To load the rifle, the ball was placed in the centre of a greased leather patch and rammed home with considerable force; initially wooden mallets were used to provide the necessary power, but they were withdrawn from service around 1803. A supply of spare greased patches was carried in a small box with a spring brass lid on the side of the rifle. The maximum rate at which perfect steady shots could be taken was reckoned to be one per minute; with the musket, up to four shots were possible. It was due to the comparative slowness of the Baker rifle that Napoleon declined to use it.

Manufacture of the Baker was slow and expensive, costing about three times that of the musket, but from 1800 to 1815, more than 30,000 rifles were produced. So that the barrel would not reflect the sun's rays, which could reveal the position of a rifleman in the field, the barrel of the Baker rifle was deliberately 'browned'. When firing the rifle, a number of practical positions included prone (lying flat), standing, sitting and kneeling. Unlike the musket, which required a volley of shots from a group of soldiers to have any chance of hitting the intended target, just a single shot from a rifle could reach a target from a far greater distance.

## Brown Bess vs Baker Rifle

|  | **Brown Bess** | **Baker Rifle** |
| --- | --- | --- |
| **Barrel (type and length)** | Smoothbore, 29–42 inches | Rifled, 30–30.5 inches |
| **Calibre** | .753, 14 balls per bag | .615–.70, 20 balls per bag |
| **Bayonet length** | 17 inches | 24 inches |
| **Weight** | 9 lb 11 oz | 9 lb 6 oz |
| **Ignition** | Flintlock | Flintlock |
| **Rate of fire** | 3–5 per minute | 1–2 per minute |
| **Accuracy** | 75–80 yards | 300 yards |
| **Sights** | None | Two |

## Bayonets
Each musket was fitted with a 16-inch bayonet of fluted steel, attached to the muzzle by a collar. A very low percentage of casualties resulted from bayonet use, although they were effective in bringing down cavalry and terrorizing the enemy. The Baker rifle was fitted with a sword bayonet that was useful in camp for lopping off branches to make shelters or to chop firewood. Bayonets also made good candlesticks.

## Swords

More usually the weapon of officers and non-commissioned officers, swords varied greatly in style from nation to nation and from unit to unit, perhaps because officers were expected to provide their own, from various different sources. British infantry swords were generally straight-bladed, but light-infantry officers wore the curved 1796-pattern, light-cavalry sabres. In Wellington's view, officers should not leave their quarters without their sword.

## Pikes

Infantry sergeants carried a pike or halberd (after the sixteenth-century weapon) measuring 7–9 feet long instead of a firearm (except in Rifle Regiments) with a 6-inch crossbar below the point to prevent over-penetration. They were also used to make a triangle to which a man was tied for a flogging. Carrying a weapon as large as the pike, accidents were inevitable. On one occasion, the NCO in the 1/7th (Royal Fusiliers) was running with his pike when he tripped, caught the point in the ground and fell forward onto the butt, which went right through his body.

## Pistols

Many officers carried pistols, but they were not as widespread in action as they were to become in later conflicts.

## INFANTRY DRILL

On the battlefield, it was essential that the infantry moved as one unit. Close order and drill, therefore, filled the life of British infantrymen from the moment they enlisted. First the soldier learned to drill without his weapon, and men who could not tell left from right often had a wisp of straw stuck under a bootlace to remember which was the 'straw foot'. Then the soldier was taught 'manual exercise', which involved learning how to load and fire his musket. He then graduated to 'platoon exercise', combining his own drill with that of a small body of men. The average soldier spent far more time engaged in learning to march with the gun than he did actually firing it. Every soldier, NCO and officer (including the commanding officer) had to learn his drill book. The regulations setting out the movements in which all units had to be trained were commonly referred to as the 'Eighteen Manoeuvres', based on rules laid out by Colonel Sir David Dundas. The three main types of infantry formation were the column, the line or the square. Each had an important part to play in battlefield tactics and required lengthy drilling so they could all be adopted quickly while in combat.

## Column

The column promoted control and was favoured particularly by the French for its manoeuvrability and the way it would maintain unit morale for longer periods under fire. A French column would advance upon an enemy position and either overwhelm it with numbers or frighten the defenders into retreating. It lacked firepower, however, as only the front ranks and troops on the outside could fire, and if a column moved against a single line of infantry that held firm – most British troops, for example – then the column was likely to be the one to break. To add musket power the French developed the *ordre mixte*, where two columns would flank and be supported by infantry in line.

## Line

The line optimized firepower. Infantry units would form lines – three for French and most continental armies, two for British – enabling all available muskets to be fired at the enemy. While effective against infantry, the line was weak against cavalry. Troops caught in the open by horsemen would usually suffer horrendous injuries. The Duke of Wellington took particular care to shelter his line behind the crest of a suitable hill where possible, and many clashes between French columns and British lines occurred when the French collided with a line that had previously been out of sight. When the enemy attacked, the British line would often remain still and silent, maintaining a quiet concentration that could be most intimidating. When the call to fire eventually came, the infantry released their charge in a long sweeping volley that ran the length of the line. Despite the inaccuracy of the musket, if the enemy was close enough, the effect of such a volley could be devastating. When the first row of the line had fired, the second row would then take over. This system would continue until the enemy were so close that bayonets were deployed. Although this seems a quite clear and straightforward process, in reality it was often much more chaotic. After a long battle the air was thick with smoke that obscured vision and stung the eyes. Discipline was vital. Often, the side that held its nerve for the longest would be the ultimate victors, with the result that in some battles, the infantry would slog it out for hour upon hour.

## Square

The square acted as the battlefield refuge for infantry under attack from opposition cavalry. It would present a hedge of bayonets to ward off the horsemen, who would in turn make use of lances or cavalry firearms.

When ordered to form a square, the infantry would come together in an oblong formation, with the front ranks jamming their musket butts into the ground to begin the process of building an almost impregnable hedge of steel. It was rare for cavalry to break a square, but when it did happen then the infantry faced certain death.

# THE ARTILLERY

The Royal Artillery was well trained and effective, although they suffered from being the target of light guns (the standard name for cannons), as well as a lack of resources. After 1800 the French artillery service benefited from the fact that their new Commander-in-Chief, Napoleon Bonaparte, was a specialized artillery officer. Combined with technological and organizational advances, the French boasted an artillery division that gave them considerable advantage over the British, which resulted in more aggressive battlefield tactics and a growing dependence on heavy guns.

In 1799 there were six British artillery battalions, rising to ten in 1808. The British artillery between 1795 and 1810 was comprised of 42 per cent Irish and 21 per cent Scottish troops, and many recruits were labourers before entering service. Being part of a gun crew was hard, noisy work. The guns recoiled each time they were fired, and had to be pushed back into position and re-aimed after each shot. To ensure they did not fire on their own troops, the artillery crew had to wait for the smoke and haze to clear, to give themselves an unobscured view of their target. However, it was often necessary simply to wait for a gap in the smoke, despite the risks involved.

Towing the artillery was a slow, heavy business, as roads were often narrow, muddy or just plain rough, especially around the Peninsula. In 1794 the Royal Regiment of Artillery formed the Corps of Artillery Drivers in response to the problems generated by contracting civilian drivers and horses to pull the guns on campaigns. Civilians were often slow to move into a battlefield and had a worrying tendency to decamp when the fighting started, leaving the artillery stranded. The introduction of the Corps of Drivers certainly brought about improvement, but the system was still far from perfect. Gunners took turns walking ahead of the column using a limber axle as a 'gauge' to make sure there was enough room for the artillery to pass through.

Where the road was too narrow, the crews had to use picks and tools to widen the rock walls and roads manually. Because of their slow progress, the artillery columns risked trailing behind the rest of the army and therefore being exposed to attacks by partisans.

The gunners were also dependent on their horses, without which the artillery units were stuck. At the Battle of Waterloo, Captain Mercer lost 140 of his 200 horses at their final deployment point. The dead horses had to be freed from their harnesses before the live ones could be re-grouped into effective teams, which took up precious time and reduced the army's efficiency.

The artillery was usually placed into a general pool of units that could then be directed towards temporary 'column' commanders. Although this often resulted in the sporadic distribution of guns, commanders could still mass artillery, as happened with the Austrians at the battle of Marengo and the Russians at Eylau. However, the French, as a part of the reorganization of the army into corps, created semi-autonomous artillery formations that were under the command of young officers. They and their generals were therefore well versed in maintaining a fast, offensive tempo on the battlefield. The British Army, in continuing to use the old pool system, was slow to react to these new methods.

## ARTILLERY WEAPONS

### Cannon

The basic guns were twelve-calibre and were usually known by the weight of shot they fired – i.e. three- or six-pounders. Nine-pounders became available during the Peninsular War. The heaviness of eighteen- and twenty-four-pounders meant these were usually employed only in sieges, where speed of movement in advance or retreat was not so great an issue. British cannon barrels were made of brass, with the carriages, wheels and limbers painted grey. Guns were mounted on 'limbers' – two-wheeled carriages for transportation – and the shot was conveyed on the 'caisson'.

## Range capability of cannon

| Gun type (calibre) | Solid shot – maximum (in metres) | Solid shot – effective (in metres) | Firing canister (in metres) |
|---|---|---|---|
| AUSTRIA | | | |
| 3-pounder | 850 | 320–400 | 275 |
| 6-pounder | 920 | 370–470 | 370 |
| 12-pounder | 1,100 | 640 | 460 |
| | | | |
| BRITAIN | | | |
| 3-pounder | 1,000 | 320–400 | 275 approx |
| 6-pounder | 1,100–1,350 | 550–640 | 320–360 |
| 9-pounder | 1,550 | 725–825 | 410 |
| | | | |
| FRANCE | | | |
| 4-pounder | 1,100 | 640 | 360 |
| 6-pounder | 1,350 | 725 | 360–410 |
| 8-pounder | 1,350 | 725 | 360–410 |
| 12-pounder | 1,350 | 725 | 460–500 |
| | | | |
| PRUSSIA | | | |
| 3-pounder | 920 | 400 | 275 |
| 6-pounder | 1,350 | 640–825 | 360 |
| 12-pounder | 1,800 | 825 | 500 |
| | | | |
| RUSSIA | | | |
| 6-pounder | 1,350 | 725 | 360 |
| 12-pounder | 1,800 | 640–825 | 460–550 |

## Cannonballs

Cannonballs, or roundshot, were solid balls of iron of varying sizes. Their range of weight – three-pounder, six-pounder or twelve-pounder – decided the guns from which they would be fired. They were aimed at various targets, including infantry, buildings and other artillery, and they whistled as they approached. The success of the cannonball would depend upon how it bounced or rolled. The ball was usually fired on a straight and direct trajectory at about chest height so that it could cut through the enemy troops; a direct hit from artillery could cut a man in two. Even when a ball landed, it would continue bouncing for some distance, crashing through the infantry divisions and breaking ankles. While a cannonball bouncing on dry ground could flatten a number of men, in wet weather the ball could just hit soggy earth and come to an immediate ineffective halt. Artillery men usually sought areas of flat, hard, open ground, devoid of obstacles or irregularities, to maximize impact.

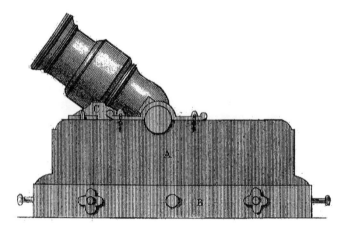

## Howitzers

These guns were used for high-angle fire, and were differentiated by their bore diameter rather than the weight of shot.

## Range capability of howitzers

| Gun type (calibre) | Solid shot – maximum (in metres) | Solid shot – effective (in metres) | Firing canister (in metres) |
|---|---|---|---|
| **AUSTRIA** 7-pounder | 1,200 | 640 | 460 |
| **BRITAIN** 5.5-inch | 1,550 | 640 | 460 |
| **FRANCE** 6-inch | 1,100 | 640 | 460–550 |
| **PRUSSIA** 7-pounder | 1,450 | 640 | 500 |
| 12-pounder | 1,800 | 640 | 500 |
| **RUSSIA** Unicorns | 1,600–2,250 | 640 | 460–550 |

### Rockets

Congreve rockets were mounted on long sticks, and would shoot a barrage of twelve-pounder explosives in the general direction of the enemy. They were used in Wellesley's attack on Copenhagen in 1807, but their erratic performance ultimately turned him against them. In January 1813 two rocket troops were added to the Royal Horse Artillery, but they did not perform well in the Peninsula, and were only included in the Waterloo attack when the gunner officer pleaded with Wellington to allow them to be used.

### Canister

Canister, or case-shot, was a lethal short-range ammunition (capable of reaching up to 250 metres) that caused maximum casualties among the enemy. Made of thin tin, the case was filled with lead balls of up to 200 grams each and would break apart upon leaving the barrel of the gun. The spread of shot could shatter enemy ranks. When using case-shot, artillery crews often positioned guns on the slight reverse of a ridge where it was difficult for the enemy to get a direct hit, and where the shot might hit the enemy troops marching uphill.

### Shells

With a thin case, the shell was fitted with a timing fuse cut so that it would explode within, or close to, large bodies of enemy troops. On disintegration it would spray shrapnel across a wide area, injuring or killing a large number of opposing troops. Explosive munitions were not widely used at the time, however, roundshot being the most common, followed by canister.

## ARTILLERY PERSONNEL

A nine-pound British cannon was manned by five soldiers who were, in order of seniority:

A SERGEANT, who commanded and aimed the gun;

THE SPONGEMAN, positioned to the right of the barrel, who wiped the gun out with a damp fleece;

THE LOADER, on the left, who placed the ammunition;

THE VENTSMAN, standing by the breech, who blocked the touch-hole;

THE FIRER, who applied a portfire to the touch-hole.

The number of crews differed between countries: in Austria, the number of gunners was six; in France there were six men for a four-pounder, eight for an eight-pounder and eight for a twelve-pounder; in Prussia, seven men were used, and in Russia, ten were employed for light artillery and twelve for heavy artillery.

## Firing Sequence

THE LOADER inserts a charge and ball into the barrel.

THE SPONGEMAN rams the ball into position.

THE VENTSMAN covers the touch-hole with his thumb to prevent any premature explosion if traces of burning particles remain from a previous shot.

THE VENTSMAN pricks the shot's cartridge, positions a firing tube in the touch-hole and checks the cannon's elevation.

When the gun is sighted, the firer touches his portfire to the tube and the cannon is then fired.

Upon firing, the gun creates a huge explosion that pushes the projectile out of the barrel and up into the air. The gun carriage is pushed back several feet by the recoil of the explosion.

The hot gun has to be 'run up' again to its original position by its crew, using handspikes and ropes.

THE SPONGEMAN dips his fleecy ramrod into a bucket of water and cleans out the barrel of the cannon to reduce the chance of sparks occurring, prior to igniting the next charge.

## BRITISH ARMY COLOURS

Made of silk and measuring 6 feet 6 inches long by 6 feet deep, and carried on a pike 9 feet 10 inches tall, colours (or, for cavalry regiments, guidons and standards) stood proudly as the heart and soul of a regiment's honour. Each cavalry regiment or infantry battalion had two colours, collectively called a 'stand'; the King's (or Queen's) colour consisted of a Union flag with the regimental badge in its centre, while the regimental colour displayed the regiment's number and badge in the centre, sometimes with a Union flag in the upper corner nearest to the staff. In the confusion of battle, men would use the colours as a rallying point, and they were defended fiercely, if not fanatically, as symbols of a regiment's honour and traditions. Such large flags were not easy to handle, and they were carried in action by the junior ensigns (as well as meaning a flag, an ensign was also the lowest rank of commissioned officer in the British Army), who were often very young; they would usually be accompanied, or at least watched over, by a guard of veteran NCOs or privates, the group being known as the 'colour party'. A battalion took enormous pride in its colours, to the extent that some of the fiercest battles raged over attempts to capture them, and the British would in turn put much effort into trying to capture an enemy's colours – eagles in the case of the French. Regiments that were successful in taking French eagles were usually given the right to incorporate them in their own badges. By the end of the eighteenth century regimental colours also began to show selected battle honours awarded for distinction in a particular battle or action (see 'Battle Honours', pages 51-2). The only infantry battalions not to carry colours were those of the rifle regiments, since they were generally deployed in small detachments, often in several different areas of the battlefield.

## BATTLE HONOURS

Regimental colours were more than just a regiment's battle flag, or a rallying point for its soldiers. They were also – and remain so to this day – historical documents on which could be read testament to the regiment's prowess, and a declaration of pride in its soldiers' martial accomplishments and those of their regimental predecessors. The army had a number of honours it could bestow on these successful regiments. Occasionally they would be awarded a title – for example, the 1st Dragoon Guards of Sharpe's day were also known as the 'King's Regiment of Dragoon Guards' – or might have appointed to them a colonel-in-chief of royal blood (colonels-in-chief are always drawn from royalty). Also, triumph in certain campaigns and engagements allowed regiments to display a symbolic badge – for example, certain regiments that distinguished themselves in the campaigns in India from 1796 to 1826 were permitted to bear, from that time on, the Royal Tiger on their colours. Further to these accolades was the battle honour, in which a regiment's distinguished action on the field – for example, at Copenhagen in 1801, in the combined land and sea attack on the Danish capital – would bring it the privilege of displaying the name of the action on their colours; occasionally, one or more battle honours would be incorporated into the regimental badge. For successful regiments, and especially those that had seen much action, these battle honours would accumulate over time, to be proudly displayed as proof of their successes and acknowledgement of approbation from the army's high command and, very often, from the Crown.

Prior to 1800, only three battle honours had been awarded: 'Namur' (1695), 'Gibraltar' (1704-5) and 'Emsdorff' (1760); after this date, however, they were granted with far greater frequency. Battle honours might mark successful skirmishes, battles and even campaigns (such as 'Egypt' [1801]), but it should be obvious that in the chaos of the field, trying to measure the 'success' of a regiment's actions, or whether one unit deserved to be honoured over another – or even determining whether a 'victory' had been achieved at all – could never have a precise measure. Thus, awarding battle honours was often an arbitrary and anomalous affair. Some regiments present at a particular engagement might be honoured, while others that played an equal or greater part neglected, and the honours could also be 'backdated', often by a century or more, so that a regiment's recognition might arrive two hundred years after the action. Despite this, battle honours were fiercely earned and proudly worn, and many of those honours won in Sharpe's time can still be seen on the regiments' colours as they exist today. (Since the British Army has fought in many more wars – including the two world wars of the twentieth century – since Sharpe's day, it is no longer possible for most regiments to display all their battle honours on their colours. As a result, a colour usually displays a representative sample of battle honours gained during the regiment's history. A further problem is that the amalgamation of regiments, mainly since the end of the Second World War, has meant that some modern units like the Royal Green Jackets, which was formed from three highly distinguished light-infantry or rifle regiments, is heir to all the battle honours won by those three regiments before amalgamation.)

## A selection of the battle honours awarded between 1797 and 1815

India* 1796–1826
Fishguard 1797 (the only battle honour for an action on
    British soil)

| | |
|---|---|
| Seringapatam 1799 | Copenhagen 1801 |
| Egypt 1801 | Monte Video 1807 |
| Vimiera 1808 | Peninsula* 1808-1814 |
| Corunna 1809 | Talavera 1809 |
| Busaco 1810 | Albuhera 1811 |
| Barrosa 1811 | Fuentes d'Oñor 1811 |
| Almaraz 1812 | Badajos 1812 |
| Detroit 1812 | Salamanca 1812 |
| Miami 1813 | Nive 1813 |
| Nivelle 1813 | Pyrenees 1813 |
| Vittoria 1813 | Bladensburg 1814 |
| Orthes 1814 | Toulouse 1814 |
| Waterloo 1815 | |

* starred entry denotes a campaign honour

## FRENCH ARMY EAGLES

The Eagle symbolized the Emperor's presence and was the rallying point in battle, of equivalent importance to the British colours. From 1804 all Eagles were personally presented by the Emperor to all guard and line regiments and therefore became objects of worship. So important were they that, in 1807, Napoleon initially ordered they be left at depot when going on campaign (an order widely ignored). In 1808 he set up special 'Eagle-bearing parties' and a new appointment – that of a *porte aigle* ranking as an ensign – was created for all infantry regiments. A veteran of ten years, these carriers were to be supported by two senior sergeants, and each member of the party was to carry a spontoon – a short sword and two pistols, carried in an open breast holster. The honour of capturing the first French Eagle of the Peninsular War went to Ensign Keogh and Sergeant Masterman of the 1/87th (now the Royal Irish Rangers) at the Battle of Barossa on 5 March 1811. No fewer than seven French officers or NCOs fell defending the Eagle. The 1/87th were subsequently known as the 'Aigle-takers', and later adopted an eagle with a wreath as a badge.

## THE CAVALRY

Wellington accused the cavalry of 'galloping at everything', but they provided an impressive and incisive fighting force on the battlefield and an effective means of communication away from it. Officers brought their own horses to war, many of which were exported from England for officers, NCOs and men, although indigenous breeds, accustomed to local conditions, usually fared better. More horses were killed by disease, maltreatment or malnutrition than by the enemy. Wellington himself ran a number of horses to death. A horse's daily rations in barracks consisted of 12 lb of hay, 10 lb of corn and 8 lb of straw, with 18 lb of hay and 8 lb of corn on campaign. Procuring adequate fodder for the army's mounts was a constant challenge for the horsemen.

**Height of the 2nd Dragoons' horses in 1813**

57 were 16 hands          256 were 15.2 hands
340 were 14.2 hands       55 were 14 hands

In battle against other cavalry, the British cavalry units would advance at speed, getting as close to the enemy as possible before drawing swords for the attack. It was common for one or both sides to hesitate before contact. Facing opposition infantry, the British cavalry would time their charge so that they could spur the final assault just after the soldiers had fired their muskets. When moving against infantry squares the British would strike at the corners of the formation to lessen the number of muskets that could be brought to bear. The perfect time for such an attack was while the infantry were trying to move, or if it had first been softened up by British artillery. Generally, if infantry held their ground, they were unlikely to concede against the cavalry.

When charging enemy guns, the British tried to make the assault in two groups. One would be the real attack force, while the other's move would be a feint to distract and draw away the attention of the gunners. Once the charge was initiated it not only had to deal with the artillery crews, but also any support troops nearby. This allowed the cavalry approaching the guns either to kill all the gunners, spike the guns with nails through the touch-holes, or capture – or kill – the artillery horses, thus rendering the artillery force immobile.

## CAVALRY ORGANIZATION

In the cavalry, the troop, commanded by a captain, was the administrative equivalent of the company. In 1800, most regiments were allowed ten troops, two of them remaining at the regimental depot and the others forming the regiment's fighting strength. Each troop had a captain, a lieutenant, a cornet, three sergeants, four corporals, a trumpeter, a farrier, and fifty to sixty rank-and-file. These troops paired off to make five squadrons. It was usual for a battalion to send four squadrons into the field and leave one squadron at home as reserves. The British cavalry was divided into three types: Household, Heavy and Light.

**Household**: The Household Regiments were the sovereign's bodyguards and so were not involved in many of the campaigns. They did, however, serve both in the Peninsula and at Waterloo.

**Heavy**: In continental armies, the heavy cavalry were termed as Cuirassiers and Heavy Dragoons, but in the British Army the heavy cavalry were the Dragoon Guards and Dragoons. Dragoon is simply a name given to mounted soldiers, which is said to have originated from the French 'Dragon' or short musket used by them, and so called because of the shape of the cocking piece. A heavy regiment would usually make heavy and decisive charges in pitched battle, using heavy war horses rather than 'light' dragoons. There were seven Dragoon Guards regiments numbered from one to seven and there were six Dragoons regiments which were classified as heavy that were numbered from one to six.

**Light**: Much of the light cavalry were involved in skirmishes and in providing communications between army encampments. In retreats they could hold off the enemy, giving the rest of the army valuable time to regroup or cover distance. The light regiments of the British Army were Dragoons regiments numbered from seven to twenty-five. In Continental armies, the light cavalry were called Lancers, Light Dragoons and Hussars. The Lancers were named after the lance that they carried – a 240-centimetre shaft with a 30-centimetre point. The Poles, Austrian Uhlans and Russian Cossacks had used these weapons for centuries and Napoleon's lancers were eminently skilled in the pursuit of fleeing infantry. With its razor-sharp blade, the lance was a most effective weapon for poking at enemy troops when they were formed in their 'squares', but Britain had no cavalry Lancers at this time. In 1806 the British Army renamed four of their Light Dragoon regiments and called them 'Hussars'. These new regiments were the 7th, 11th, 15th and 18th, but the change to Hussar (a fifteenth-century Hungarian word meaning 'one in twenty', relating to the conscription of one man in twenty from every village) was really only a change in name and uniform.

## CAVALRY WEAPONS

### Sabres

The British cavalry carried sabres, of which there were two main styles – the 1796 pattern light-cavalry sabre and the straight-bladed 1796 heavy-cavalry sabre. Unwieldy and poorly balanced, the 1796 patterns were generally used as hacking weapons. While they would cause terrible wounds, the use of the edge of the blade rather than the point resulted in fewer killing strokes. In contrast French horsemen preferred to use the points of their swords and run the enemy through so there was a large disparity in casualties between the two styles. The French suffered more horrific wounds, while the British initially experienced more deaths.

## CAVALRY EQUIPMENT IN CAMP

| Item | Per Cavalry Regiment of 8 Troops |
|---|---|
| Canteen and straps | 1 per man |
| Haversacks | 1 per man |
| Blankets | 1 per man |
| Bill hooks | 1 per 10 men |
| Camp kettles | 1 per 10 men |
| Sets of forage cords | 4 per set/half set per horse |
| Picquet ropes | 1 per 9 horses |
| Water buckets | 1 per 12 horses |
| Nosebags: hair | 1 per horse |
| Cornsacks | 1 per horse |
| Saddle water decks | 1 per horse (not issued to Hussars) |
| Reaping hooks | 10 per troop |
| Spades | 1 per troop |
| Shovels | 1 per squadron |
| Pickaxes | 1 per squadron |
| Felling axes | 1 per squadron |
| Public mules | 14 per regiment |
| Pack saddles | 14 per regiment |
| Bridles and collars with winkers | 14 per regiment |
| Medicine panniers | 4 per regiment |
| Sergeant armourer's panniers | 2 per regiment |
| Sergeant saddler's panniers | 2 per regiment |
| Baggage straps for paymaster | 1 set per regiment |

## ENGINEERS

The history of military engineers in, first, English, and then British, service spans more than nine hundred years, dating back to the eleventh century and the arrival of William the Conqueror, who brought with him engineers from France.

Since sieges formed a major part of warfare from the earliest times until well into the nineteenth century, engineers skilled not only in breaching fortresses, but in their defence, were extremely important in any major campaign. The black arts of sapping – constructing tunnels or trenches to conceal an attacking force's approach – and mining – constructing tunnels to be filled with explosives in order to breach or bring down a fortification – had been in existence almost since gunpowder became a commonplace on European battlefields; Shakespeare's Hamlet, speaking of his enemies, reflects upon how it is 'sport to have the enginer / Hoist with his own petar' – that is, blown up by his own explosive charge – and continues, 'I will delve one yard below their mines, / And blow them at the moon.'

What became the Corps of Royal Engineers had its origins in the establishment of the Board of Ordnance in the fifteenth century. As a result, the part that engineers have played in the success of this country's armed forces is arguably unsurpassed by any other arm or service. In 1717 a Corps of Engineers – consisting entirely of officers – was formed as part of the Board of Ordnance, and in 1787 was granted a royal title (the title that it has to this day). In 1757 a Corps of Royal Military Artificers and Labourers was formed by granting military status to what had previously been a civilian corps formed in 1722, and in 1787 this became the Corps of Royal Military Artificers; consisting entirely of other ranks, its officers were provided by the Corps of Royal Engineers. (In fact, the first permanent engineer soldiers – as opposed to officers – in the British Army appeared with the formation of a Soldier Artificer Company in Gibraltar in 1772; this was absorbed into the Royal Military Artificers in 1797.) In

1812, the Royal Military Artificers became the Corps of Royal Sappers and Miners, and remained thus until 1855 when the Board of Ordnance was abolished and it was amalgamated with the Corps of Royal Engineers under the latter title.

Despite the long history of engineers in warfare, it was the Peninsular War that especially highlighted the need for a trained body of field or combat engineers. In 1812, on the authority of Wellington himself, Major Charles Pasley, RE, formed a school for this purpose at Chatham, and the first trainees of this new institution were sent on active service in Spain in 1813 and 1814. It continues today as the Royal School of Military Engineering.

Thus Wellington's army in Spain and France drew engineer officers and other ranks from two corps, although officers from the Royal Engineers also served in an individual capacity, advising and overseeing operations. Since much of their work of surveying or assessing defences or positions took them within gunshot of the enemy, they suffered very high casualties: almost 25 per cent of the 102 officers who served in the Peninsula were killed or died of wounds. They played a vital role in the reduction of enemy-held fortresses such as those at Badajoz and Ciudad Rodrigo, although static siege warfare could take a dreadful toll of both attackers and engineers, not only in terms of casualties, but in terms of health and morale, as soldiers were confined to trenches around the besieged fortress.

The Corps of Royal Engineers has no battle honours. Its motto '*Ubique*' ('Everywhere'), awarded by King William IV in 1836, is particularly appropriate, however, in view of the corps's involvement in every major military campaign and peacetime operation since the eighteenth century.

## TRANSPORT AND SUPPLY

The practical considerations of launching and maintaining a large-scale military campaign – overseas and on several fronts – were an enormous logistical challenge for the commanders of Wellington's armies. To ensure the army operated at maximum efficiency in the Peninsula and France it was essential that the men received continuous supplies of rations, bedding, clothing, weaponry and ammunition, both to equip the soldiers sufficiently well to enable them to do their job, and to ensure a certain 'standard of living' to keep up morale. The army in the field also needed replacements and reinforcements, not least to replace men killed or wounded in battle, and the many who fell sick.

With the retreating enemy forces often stripping great swaths of land of food and fodder as they withdrew, the British Army could not rely on living off the land – something which, in any case, was hampered by Wellington's strictures against looting: what was taken must be paid for. The first concerted effort to introduce a corps specifically to oversee the transport of supplies came with the establishment, under the Board of Ordnance, of the Corps of Waggoners in 1794, manned primarily by released prisoners inexperienced in handling horses, which quickly gave the corps a bad reputation. Indeed, the unit was abolished after failing to supply adequately the Duke of York's expedition against France in 1795, and following a number of abortive attempts to introduce a replacement service during the next seven years, the Royal Wagon Train was finally established in 1802. While many regiments would continue to maintain their own transportation, as had been the case before 1794, this marked the beginnings of a corps which, after passing through several reforms and incarnations, would eventually become the Royal Army Service Corps (from 1965 the Royal Corps of Transport, which was later subsumed in today's Royal Logistics Corps).

Transportation in Sharpe's day relied almost entirely on horses, mules and wagons. To keep the front line supplied with victuals, armament and clothing, merchant and Royal Navy vessels would offload at ports in northern Spain, France and Portugal, and from there the goods would be stored in depots before being sent on by road; replacements and reinforcements generally marched to join their units. The standard wagon was made of wood and had rudimentary suspension, but was unable to carry heavy loads. Often, the ranks of the Royal Wagon Train would be swelled by local cart drivers and pack animals in an attempt to keep up with the demand upon the corps's resources. This demand was not well served by the innate corruption that was often prevalent in the supply network; many soldiers were court-martialled for looting their own supplies, and some of those in charge of distribution would sell supplies to the highest bidder.

Since overseeing supply and transport was primarily the responsibility of the Commissariat – civilians 'appointed to their office on the king's authority, although not holding his commission', as Wellington put it – the prevalence of this corruption depended largely upon the competency and honesty of these individuals. Yet while it may seem that serving in the transport corps was a tedious and unglamorous role, it was absolutely vital, and could be fraught with danger. While under intense enemy fire during the Battle of Waterloo, for instance, a Private Joseph Brewster of the Royal Wagon Train resupplied a crucial position with ammunition and ensured that it could continue fighting.

A final, gruesome responsibility of the Royal Wagon Train was transporting the dead and wounded. One can only imagine the agony that a rocking and pitching wagon would cause to a soldier suffering from gunshot or bayonet wounds as he was transported over the unmade roads of India or Spain.

## A heavy load

From 1805 a wood-framed, canvas knapsack designed by the army contractor John Trotter came into service. It was 18 inches broad, 13 inches high and 4 inches deep, but by no means easy to carry, as Rifleman Benjamin Harris found in 1808:

> The weight I myself toiled under was tremendous, and I often wondered at the strength I possessed at this period, which enabled me to endure it; for indeed, I am convinced that many of our infantry sank and died under the weight of their knapsacks alone. For my own part, being a handicraft I marched under a weight sufficient to impede the free motions of a donkey; for beside my well-filled kit, there was the great-coat rolled on top, my blanket and camp kettle, my haversack, stuffed full of leather for repairing the men's shoes, together with a hammer and other tools... ship-biscuit and beef for three days. I also carried my canteen filled with water, my hatchet and rifle, and eighty rounds of ball cartridge in my pouch; this last, except the beef and biscuit, being the best thing I owned, and which I always gave the enemy the benefit of when proximity offered.

Officers invariably brought more equipment with them on campaigns but, with the exception of Sir John Moore's 1808 Peninsular campaign, when he ordered officers to carry their own kit, officers could buy a packhorse or rely on the regiment to carry what they brought.

**Weights of load, minus saddle and equipment (in pounds)**

| | |
|---|---|
| Man | 50 |
| Donkey | 100 |
| Pack bullocks | 160 |
| Horses and mules | 160–200 |
| Camels | 320–400 |
| Elephants | 800–1,200 |
| Light cart, drawn by a horse or mule | 500–600 |
| Cart, drawn by two horses or mules | 1,000 |
| Light wagon, team of four horses or mules | 1,600–2,000 |
| Wagon, team of six horses or mules | 3,000 |
| Cart, drawn by two bullocks | 850 |
| Cart, drawn by four bullocks | 1,600 |

## SIEGES

The British fought four sieges in the course of the Peninsular War – at Ciudad Rodrigo, Badajoz and Burgos (the latter both featured in *Sharpe's Company*), and San Sebastian. Despite being an immense drain on time, money and human life, sieges were often necessary; an enemy fort could not be ignored during wartime, since it threatened an advancing army's supply lines and communication. Sometimes a city was blockaded by a force that an advancing army had left behind specifically to maintain supply lines and prevent enemy soldiers from relieving the garrison. Soldiers generally hated sieges, as George Gleig recounts:

'There is no species of duty in which the soldier is liable to be employed, so galling or disagreeable as a siege. Not that it is deficient in cause of excitement, which, on the contrary, are in hourly operation; but it ties him so completely down to the spot, and breaks in so repeatedly upon his hours of rest, and exposes him constantly to danger, and that too at times and places where no honour is to be gained, that we cannot greatly wonder at the feelings of absolute hatred which generally prevail, among the privates at least of a besieging army, against the garrison which does its duty to its country by holding out to the last extremity.'

## Principal sieges during Wellington's career

Seringapatam, May 1799
Gawilghur, November 1803
Copenhagen, September 1807
Ciudad Rodrigo, January 1812
Badajoz, April 1812
Burgos, September–October 1812
San Sebastian, June–August 1813

## Siege procedures

When a siege was deemed necessary, the plan of action was clear: The attacker first secured his own logistic base – the siege park – to create a blockade of the fort under siege, which prevented relieving forces, communication, food or support from outside.

Engineers began to dig trenches around the fort known as 'parallels' (so called because they ran parallel to the walls of the fort). The first parallel was built some distance from the fort, out of range of the defender's guns. The engineers then drove zig-zag trenches forward in a line called 'saps' (from which the term 'sapper' is derived), and continued until they reached the required place to open a second and third parallel.

The second and then third parallels were built progressively closer to the fort. At this stage batteries were brought in to try and dislodge the enemy pieces on bastions. Infantry were often used to help the engineers with the heavy shifting of dirt. At Badajoz, during 28–29 March, the duty division had to provide working parties of 1,000 men by day and 1,200 men by night. If the attacking force had the time, and the ground conditions were right, engineers might also dig a tunnel beneath the defences in order to lay mines.

Once the trenches were ready, siege guns could be brought in at close range to batter the walls for a breach. These guns were often heavier than the six- or twelve-pound guns favoured on the battlefield, and consequently were far less easily manoeuvrable. They steadily pounded the base of the wall, opening a long groove.

If the artillery managed to blast a hole in the fort wall that could be breached, an important decision had to be made. The rules of war dictated that the governor now had to surrender or else no quarter might be given to the garrison or the city, resulting in a sack. Since the opposing forces were likely to be victorious once the wall was breached, the decision to surrender might save both property and lives, but nothing was certain and sometimes a governor would remain resolute in defence of his land.

If the opposing army stormed the fort then it usually did so on a number of fronts to split the inner defences and to try to weaken at least one area. As well as storming the breach, the attackers might also use escalade (scaling ladders), as was the case at Badajoz, or distract internal forces away from the breach in feint attacks. Usually a successful attack relied on all three tactics.

The first party to storm the breach was known as the 'Forlorn Hope'. Any soldier involved in this highly dangerous force would become an instant hero, and if the siege was a success the officer in charge might expect a promotion. In the Peninsula, there was great competition for places in the first assault, in spite of the extreme danger, and lots were drawn to choose the 'lucky' men. In the French armies, such men, called 'enfants perdu' (lost children), received the Legion of Honour.

During a breach the defending force might use sharp spikes of caltrops and planks studded with nails, trenches with swords and knives strewn at the bottom, mines, shells and grenades, fire-balls and powder barrels to protect their property. *Chevaux-de-frise* – sword blades attached to a rotating length of timber to cut up people trying to charge in – were put to particularly lethal use by the defenders at Ciudad Rodrigo.

Once inside the breached garrison, the attacking army could be merciless. Indeed the brutal sacking of Ciudad Rodrigo, Badajoz and San Sebastian remain a stain on the British Army's record.

## AMMUNITION AND GUNS USED AT THE SIEGE OF CIUDAD RODRIGO, JANUARY 1812

| Item | On hand at start of siege | Expended/Destroyed |
|---|---|---|
| GUN: 24-pounder | 32 | 1 |
| GUN: 18-pounder | 2 | 0 |
| AMMUNITION: 24-pounder rounds | Unknown | 8,950 |
| AMMUNITION: 18-pounder rounds | Unknown | 565 |
| BARRELS OF GUNPOWDER (90 pounds) | Unknown | 834 |
| ENTRENCHING TOOLS | 2,200 | Unknown |
| SANDBAGS | 30,000 | Unknown |
| FASCINES | 600 | Unknown |
| GABIONS | 1,100 | Unknown |

## ARMY UNIFORM

Wellington was never much interested in dress. 'I think it indifferent how a soldier is clothed,' he once wrote in a letter to the Horse Guards, 'provided it is in a uniform manner, and that he is forced to keep himself clean and smart, as a soldier ought to be.' Some visitors to his camp were surprised to find his officers in a variety of different coloured jackets, and others were astonished at the disorderliness of the place. 'Had it not been known for a fact, no one would have suspected that the [General Wellington] was quartered in the town,' wrote one German commissary. 'There was no throng of scented staff officers with plumed hats, orders and stars, no main guard, no crowd of contractors, actors, valets, cooks, mistresses, equipages, horses, forrage and baggage wagons, as there is at a French or Russian headquarters.' While the Duke could be seen on the battlefield in his plain blue overcoat, others were even more eccentric. Picton, who was at the forefront of the siege of Ciudad Rodrigo and was eventually shot through the head at Waterloo, wore ragged coats and a top hat, and old clothes in varying colours and states of disrepair.

### The redcoat

Black felt, stovepipe shako hat with peak, chinstrap and oval brass plate.

Redcoat: waist-length in front with short skirts at the back; pewter buttons grouped in two; broad oblong of white worsted lace framing the button holes.

High collar. Leather stock (a despised collar that chafed the skin).

Deep yellow cuffs, trimmed with more white lace.

Two white crossbelts, one for bayonet, the other for cartridge box.

White breeches and long, tightly buttoned gaiters gave way to loose-fitting, comfortable blue/grey trousers.

Square-toed black boots with one fitting – the same for left and right.

Greatcoat.

## The rifleman

Black felt, stovepipe shako hat with peak, chinstrap and white-metal bugle-horn badge. Also green shako cord.

Short, dark green (rudimentary camouflage) jacket with three rows of nine white-metal buttons but no lace.

High collar. Leather stock (the 95th did not discard them until 1913).

Black leather belts and accoutrements.

Loose-fitting, comfortable blue/grey trousers.

Square-toed black boots.

Greatcoat.

## Hair

Throughout the eighteenth century, men wore their hair slicked back with candle-grease, 'clubbed' into a thick pony-tail that was held by a polished leather strap, and powdered. One soldier remembers the leather strap being pulled so tight that 'it was impossible to wink so much as an eyelid'. The process took up to an hour and those soldiers who were not married took it in turn to do each other's. In the Napoleonic Wars, rules on hairdressing changed considerably. Powdering was abolished in 1795, although it continued much longer in some regiments. The tight pony-tail was in turn abolished in 1808, but the regimental wives in particular objected. The reason for this was that a woman who was good with her husband's hair would not be short of suitors if she should happen to find herself widowed. If she did not have the opportunity to demonstrate her hairdressing skills, she might lose some of her appeal.

## PITCHING CAMP

When on campaign in the Peninsula, all ranks slept in bivouacs, tents or billets.

### Bivouacs

Bivouacs simply meant sleeping in the open and finding what shelter one could. The location for the camp would be determined in advance and the best spots would be chosen by seniority; trees for the officers, and bushes, grass and stones for the men. Conditions on a cold night in Spain could be lethal; sometimes dead bodies were found frozen to the ground by dawn. Often, the men would not bother trying to sleep, but huddle around a fire instead.

The British blanket was crucial for keeping warm during miserable nights outside in the cold, but it was some time before the army created the innovative British Army Blanket Tents. Blankets were often used as rudimentary tentage to keep out wind and rain. An illustration of this can be seen in the memoirs of Sergeant John Douglas of the Royal Scots: 'Our tents were very simple, soon pitched and as easily packed up. [Each tent] consisted of two blankets, two firelocks and four bayonets. At each corner of the blanket a hole was worked similar to a buttonhole, and in the centre another. A firelock stood at each end, to serve as poles. The bayonet of these firelocks passed through the corner holes of both blankets, a ramrod secured the top, and a bayonet at each end fastened in the ground completed our house.'

It wasn't until the end of 1812 that blankets were specifically converted so they could be used as emergency tents. The Portuguese army was already fitting small loops at each corner of their large blankets so that they could be tied up at night, and for the Vitória campaign in 1813, Wellington himself directed orders for the modification of blankets: 'The Officers' commanding regiments should have the corners and outside selvage of the soldiers' blankets strengthened, in order that the soldiers may pitch them, without injury to the blankets, in case it should... be necessary in order to shelter them from the sun'. Where the official blanket tents were not available, improvisation of ordinary blankets continued; at Waterloo, the blanket tent was still being issued to the army.

## Tents

Conical 'bell' tents with a nine-foot centre pole, weighing 43 pounds, were introduced in March 1813. There was one for each field officer (majors and above), one for the company officers (up to three) and one each for the adjutant, quartermaster, paymaster, and the medical staff. NCOs and men got three per company. This meant forty-seven tents for a full-strength battalion, or twenty per tent. Soldiers slept with their feet in the centre and so full were the tents that they had to move on the agreed command of 'turn'!

## Billets

A nearby town or village might provide officers and soldiers with more comfortable temporary quarters than bivouacs or tents. Homes, churches, monasteries and barns were all used, but the officers were often given the best rooms, the ordinary soldiers left to sleep on straw in a draughty corridor. Sometimes – especially in cities like Madrid or Salamanca – the quarters could be luxurious.

## THE MESS

In the Peninsular War, the regimental mess was the centre of the officer's life when he was not on duty. It provided food, lodging and – perhaps most importantly – company, rather like a club. The services offered by the mess varied according to the regiment, location and year; no two messes were alike. Inns were preferred because they usually had numerous rooms, a wine cellar and a kitchen, but churches, large houses, and barns were also used. On special days, such as Christmas, the King's birthday, National Saint's days or the night before a campaign, the officers would get together to celebrate in the mess, perhaps the most famous occasion being that of the officers of the 95th Rifles who in August 1813 got together to celebrate their regiment's tenth anniversary. On the Vera heights, in full sight of the French, seventy-three officers from the three battalions of the regiment sat down in a crude hut made from the branches of trees. Tables and benches were made by digging a trench for the officers to dangle their legs in. Although accounts of the amount of food available vary, all those who attended enjoyed the evening immensely. Lieutenant Johnny Kincaid wrote: '. . . the earth almost quaked with the weight of the feast, and the enemy certainly did, from the noise of it. For so many fellows holding such precarious tenures of their lives could not meet together in commemoration of such an event, without indulging in an occasional cheer – not a whispering cheer, but one that echoed far and wide into the French lines, and as it was a sound that had often pierced them before, and never yet boded them any good, we heard afterwards that they were kept standing at their arms the greater part of the night . . .'

The primary source of food and drink was the issued ration, but officers would, wherever possible, supplement the rations with local purchases, hunting, foraging, packages from home, from captured French stocks, or, as a last resort, from enlisted soldiers. The mess allowed the junior officers to pool whatever resources they did have, save money and share the good fortune of extra rations between them. More than anything, however, the mess provided somewhere to relax and unwind with their peers, which was so essential to creating an *esprit de corps*.

## ARMY FOOD

The Duke of Wellington never cared much for food, often surviving for a whole day on just the crust and boiled egg he sometimes stuffed in his pocket when he went riding. In his view, dinners were more occasions for company and conversation, and he rarely dined alone. The wine at his table was better than most others in the British Army and he always made sure there was plenty to go round. Although his soldiers were frequently hungry – their accounts often attest to their lack of food in the Peninsular War – Wellington did all he could to keep his army fed and watered. He took pride in the belief that they had never been reduced to eating horsemeat (unlike the French at Fuentes de Oñoro) and wrote it was 'very necessary to attend to all this detail of proper food supply and to trace a biscuit from its being landed at a Peninsula port into the man's mouth, and to provide for its removal from place to place, by land or by water'.

In the Peninsula, Wellington made a firm base in Portugal so that he could guarantee a constant supply of rations by sea and mule. Private Wheeler wrote: 'It is a mystery to thousands how we were supplied so regular as we were… If England should require the service of her army again, let me have "Old Nosey" to command. Our interests would be sure to be looked into… and we should always be as well supplied with rations as the nature of the service would admit.'

For the average soldier, breakfast consisted of bread and a small cup of beer, which was a weaker, barely-alcoholic variety, brewed largely to make water safe and drinkable. The main meal of boiled beef, boiled potatoes and beef broth was eaten between midday and two in the afternoon. When oatmeal was added to the broth it became a thin gruel known as 'skilly'. Cooking for ten men was carried out in a Flanders iron kettle that required the burning of a whole tree or a church door for its contents to be brought to the boil. On foreign campaigns, the local cooking techniques were sometimes a cause for concern, as Alexander Alexander, a garrison artilleryman in Ceylon, describes: '… our food was not only bad in itself, but cooked by the black cooks belonging to the garrison, in the most dirty and careless manner and we, being strangers in their country, could not alter their slovenly fashions. When the meat was brought to the cooking place, it was thrown down upon a dirty mat, and chopped up. Then [the] cooks sat down upon their hams, placing a knife between their toes, and cut it up into small pieces, and thus daubed all about, and without even being washed, it was boiled in curry.' Tobacco was relished as a bulwark against hunger and loneliness, and the luxury of a pound of tobacco and a pipe sold for 6s 6d.

## RATIONS IN BARRACKS

| Item | Amount |
| --- | --- |
| Flour, bread | 1.5 lbs (680g) |
| Beef or pork | 1 lb (225g) |
| Peas | 1/4 pint (150ml) |
| Butter or cheese | 1 oz (28g) |
| Rice | 1 oz (28g) |

Women assigned to the regiment were officially allocated half the men's ration, and children were issued one quarter.

## RATIONS ON CAMPAIGN

| Item | Amount |
| --- | --- |
| Bread | 1.5 lbs (680g) |
| Beef or mutton | 1 lb (225g) |
| Unground wheat or potatoes | 2lb (450g) |
| Wine (or rum) | 1 pint (600ml) (or 1/3 pint (200ml)) |

## ALCOHOL CONSUMPTION

Wellington was quoted as saying that his men 'have all enlisted for drink', and the army gained a reputation as being hard drinkers with an appetite for strong beer, brandy, wine or rum – in fact, anything they could find. Troops and officers alike did little to dispel such preconceptions.

On Wellington's retreat to Portugal in the autumn of 1812 he led his troops through the wine country of Valladolid, at the time when the tanks and vats were full of newly fermented wines. 'The conduct of some of the men would have disgraced savages,' wrote Private Wheeler. Those too drunk to walk were carried by mules and some of those too drunk to move were found drowned in the bottom of wine vats. Alcohol was also the cause of rowdiness and indiscipline, and stiff penalties were handed down to those who committed offences; with the result that careers were ruined and many lives were lost. Thomas Pococke of the 71st commented that, 'the great fault of our soldiers… was an inordinate desire for spirits of any kind. They sacrificed their life and safety for drink'. It was a feature of the age that drink ruined many a good man.

However, it was also the case that alcohol gave men 'Dutch courage' (an army expression taken from the consumption of genever, a Dutch gin, by British soldiers fighting in the Low Countries in the seventeenth century). It helped them to face battles and to get them through sometimes cold and miserable nights. Sergeant Botley served out rum from a camp skillet at the siege of Badajoz while the company were under fire, and, on the night before Waterloo, a member of the Coldstream Guards received alcoholic comfort throughout the wet night: 'I, with another officer, had a blanket, and, with a little more gin, we kept up well.' In the army, alcohol was used from beginning to end; from the moment of enrolment, when potential new recruits were plied with rum or porter, right up to the moment they went under the surgeon's knife. Drink acted as both an energizer and an anaesthetic.

## A DRINKING SONG FROM SHARPE'S ARMY DAYS

Occasionally, communal drinking was accompanied by a song, with each man taking a line, sung as a round:

> *To-whit, to-whoo*
> *To whom drinks't thou?*
> *O knave, to thee*
> *This song is well sung, I make you a vow*
> *And here's a knave that drinkest now.*

## BRANDY, O

> *A landlady of France,*
> *She loved an officer, 'tis said,*
> *And this officer he dearly loved her brandy, O!*
> *Sighed she, 'I love this officer,*
> *Although his nose is red,*
> *And his legs are what his regiment call bandy, O!'*
>
> *But when the bandy officer*
> *Was ordered to the coast,*
> *How she tore her lovely locks that looked so sandy, O!*
> *'Adieu, my soul,' says she,*
> *'If you write, pray pay the post,*
> *But before we part, let's take a drop of brandy, O!'*
>
> *She filled him out a bumper*
> *Just before he left the town,*
> *And another for herself, so neat and handy, O!*
> *So they kept their spirits up*
> *By pouring spirits down,*
> *For love is like the colic – cured by brandy, O!*

## BRITISH GENERALS (1797–1815)

Sir Charles von Alten (1764–1846)
William Carr, Viscount Beresford (1768–1854)
Sir John Colborne, 1st Baron Seaton (1778–1863)
Sir Galbraith Lowry Cole (1772–1842)
Robert Craufurd (1764–1812)
Thomas Graham, Baron Lynedoch (1748–1843)
Rowland Hill, Lord Hill (1772–1842)
Sir James Kempt (1764–1854)
John Gaspard LeMarchant (1766–1812)
Charles Gordon Lennox, Lord March, later 5th Duke
Richmond
   (1791–1860)
Sir John Moore (1761–1809)
Sir George Murray (1772–1846)
William Napier (1785–1860)
Sir Denis Pack (1772–1823)
Sir Edward Pakenham (1778–1815)
Sir Thomas Picton (1758–1815)
Sir Brent Spencer (1760–1828)
Sir William Stewart (1774–1827)
Henry Paget, 2nd Earl of Uxbridge and (1815) Marquess of
Anglesey
   (1768–1854)
Sir John Ormsby Vandeleur (1763–1849)
Sir Arthur Wellesley, later, the Duke of Wellington (1769–1852)

## ARMY INTELLIGENCE

Gathering intelligence is vital in war, and Wellington needed detailed and up-to-date reports on topographical and operational intelligence for the land that lay ahead, and on the state and tactics of the enemy at any particular time. Wellington wrote: 'All the business of war, and indeed all the business of life, is to endeavour to find out what you don't know by what you do: that's what I called "guessing what was at the other side of the hill".'

Sources of intelligence included:
    guerrillas and the local population
    cavalry or light division patrols and pickets (guards)
    captured despatches
    deserters
    prisoners
    spies, employed as 'correspondents'
    'exploring' or 'observing' officers

These 'exploring' officers would go deep into enemy territory, alone or with a handful of companions, and work their way into the local population. In *Sharpe's Gold*, it is a Major Kearsay who guides Sharpe on his mission to make contact with the local guerrillas. In history, such men included Sir John Waters, Patrick Curtis, John Grant (one of the few officers who considered himself a spy and went undercover out of uniform) and Colquhoun Grant, the most celebrated exploring officer of all, whom the guerrillas called '*Granto el Bueno*' (Grant the Good). When Grant was captured in April 1812, Wellington offered $2,000 for his rescue, remarking subsequently, 'He was worth a brigade to me'. After a series of adventures, Grant eventually escaped from France and went on to become Wellington's chief intelligence officer behind French lines during the Waterloo campaign.

## ARMY DISCIPLINE

Discipline was essential to maintain the uniformity expected of each company and battalion in Wellington's army. The truth was that the majority of British soldiers – perhaps 90 per cent – were honourable and well behaved, but given the sometimes deplorable behaviour of troops and their propensity for drinking and looting, it is hardly surprising Wellington was sometimes severe. Nor was it just the rank and file who misbehaved, as many officers indulged in drink, womanizing and violence. However the penalties for those with a commission were generally less severe, something about which Wellington himself was particularly incensed.

Many of the men in Wellington's army came from the poorest sections of society – 'the scum of the earth' as he put it – and he saw that discipline was essential to keeping such men in check. Soldiers suspected of breaking the military code were judged by three types of court martials – regimental, district or general – whose powers varied. Wellington's judge-advocate general, Francis Seymour Larpent, was meticulous in overseeing court martials during the Peninsula campaign. There was a provost marshal at Wellington's headquarters and an assistant on the staff of every division, which was in charge of prisoners to be tried by general court martial. The provost's mounted patrols were mobile and ruthless. Once in the field of operations, justice was often swift and brutal. Punishments ranged from simple detention – for example, 'riding the wooden horse' (sitting astride a sharp wooden frame) – to flogging or even the death sentence. The riflemen had their own punishments that included confining soldiers to barracks, with or without 'coat turning', which involved the offender being taken into the tailor's shop and having the letter 'C' sewn on his right sleeve, at a charge of two-pence, or the offender might be confined in the guardroom cell (called a 'black hole') for a maximum of eight days. Harsh, public punishments were seen as a deterrent, and were in keeping with the contemporary attitude to crime; even in civilian criminal law there were over two hundred capital offences in 1800.

## Flogging

Many officers viewed corporal punishment as essential for keeping a depraved core of blackguards in check. It was employed for everything from drunkenness to insolence and had the added benefit of being demonstrative and keeping the offender within his regiment. When being flogged, the guilty soldier was brought on to the parade ground, ordered to strip and tied to a large iron triangle made up of sergeants' halberds. Short whips called 'cat o' nine tails' were on hand, together with a bucket of water, a chair, a hospital orderly and the regimental surgeon. The drum major (for infantry units) or the farrier major (for the cavalry) dealt the blows, with the sergeant major calling out each stroke. Sentences varied from 25 strokes (the minimum) to 1,200 (the maximum permitted, which was calculated to kill most men). This latter punishment was reserved for desertion to the enemy, robbery with violence, or striking an officer. As the punishment continued, floggers were replaced as they grew tired and the whips exchanged as they became worn or clogged with blood and tissue. It was an unpleasant spectacle that caused many to vomit or faint. Death sometimes resulted from such an ordeal, despite the presence of a surgeon who was meant to stop the punishment it there were signs that the soldier's life was in danger. However, the transgressor had to receive the remainder when pronounced fit. In theory, if a soldier died under the lash, the sentence was to be completed on his lifeless corpse.

## Execution

Deserting to the enemy was a crime punishable by firing squad. When condemned to be shot, the disgraced soldier, his hands tied, was escorted in slow time along the front ranks of his comrades, led by a band playing the Dead March. The provost blindfolded the prisoner before pinning a white paper mark above his heart. The brigade-major read the sentence, the chaplain said a prayer, the provost motioned with his cane and the firing party fired a volley. Often a second firing squad would be available to finish off those who had not been killed outright.

All other capital crimes were punishable by hanging. In France, for instance, when Spanish troops abused the local French people, Wellington ordered his officers to hang anyone who was found committing an offence. In one case, a soldier was caught stealing apples from a French cottage and was duly strung up outside the house with an apple in his mouth to deter similar looters.

## Civil strife

There was also another reason for the need for discipline in Wellington's eyes other than to aid the cohesion of his fighting unit. There were few things that rankled him quite so much as civil strife, and this led to his insistence on fair treatment of the local people. As governor of Mysore, he had witnessed 'scenes of villainy which would disgrace the Newgate Calendar', and although he had a low regard for many of the people in whose countries he served – including India, Portugal and Spain – he remained respectful to the local feelings and interests of native peoples. In Spain, for example, when two soldiers were found looting a shop and assaulting a woman, and Wellington had satisfied himself of their guilt, he turned to the provost-marshal and said, 'In ten minutes report to me that these two men have been executed.' The bodies were still hanging there when the French under Junot entered the town, and when the French general discovered the soldiers' crime, he commented, '*Ma Foi! La discipline anglaise est bien sévère.*' ('Indeed! English discipline is very harsh.')

## CHAPLAINS

Although the word 'chaplain' originated in the twelfth century, clergymen have been involved in warfare for many centuries, whether as ministers, or as military leaders. Archbishop Turpin fought gallantly alongside Roland and Oliver against the Moors at Roncevaux in 778, and several medieval popes led armies in the field. Yet although the history of the military chaplaincy is both long and distinguished, it was not until 1796 that a more formal and recognized organization was set up by Royal Warrant under King George III. Prior to then, regiments had engaged their own chaplains, who held a commission from the Crown but were paid by their parent units. The establishment of the Army Chaplains' Department (it gained the prefix 'Royal' in 1919) put an end to regimentally engaged chaplains; instead, chaplains were attached to troops on campaign or in foreign garrisons, while at home civilian clergy were given a sum of money to minister to troops in garrison towns. The Royal Warrant establishing the department ordained that 'Chaplains shall be appointed according to the number of the Corps, in the proportion of one to each Brigade, or to every three or four Regiments.' Each chaplain in Wellington's army, therefore, held services for, and ministered to the moral and spiritual welfare of, some 3,000 to 4,000 men, when battalions were at full strength.

Yet although chaplains were comparatively well paid, they were in relatively short supply in the Peninsular campaign. Nor did they always behave in the manner expected of men of the cloth. Private William Wheeler of the 51st, whose collected letters form one of the finest records of that campaign as seen from the ranks, lamented that 'their mode of living do not agree with the doctrine they preach . . . If these Reverend Gentlemen were stationed at the sick depots and made to attend the hospitals they would be much more usefully employed than following the army with their brace of dogs and gun, running down hares and shooting partridges etc.' Some chaplains showed a marked preference for the company of a regiment's officers, rather than tending to the other ranks, and there were a number who displayed decidedly more venal traits, and who gained reputations for gluttony, drunkenness, and womanizing – and sometimes all three.

From the establishment of the department until some years after the end of the Napoleonic Wars, chaplains were drawn exclusively from the Church of England rather than the Roman Catholic or other churches, something that often caused resentment, especially among the Irish and Highland elements serving within the British Army at the time, many – if not the majority – of whom were Catholics. In an age when religious faith was not thought to be in any way out of the ordinary, and when the burden of proof for the existence, or otherwise, of God still rested with unbelievers rather than, as today, with believers, soldiers of non-Anglican denominations would often hold religious meetings among themselves. On the whole Wellington tolerated this, although he voiced a warning, referring to Methodists, that it might lead to indiscipline if soldiers began to question the virtue of their officers. Church parades were held regularly and were usually compulsory, and that too could lead to resentment among ordinary soldiers, especially non-Anglicans. None the less, it was an era in which ordinary people were well schooled in the Scriptures, even if they could not read and write, and bibles and other religious texts were commonly found among soldiers' personal effects. Respect for other faiths or denominations was not always strong, however, and despite Wellington's well-remarked – and often harshly enforced – strictures against looting and pillage, churches, convents and other religious sites in Spain and elsewhere sometimes suffered at the hands of troops bent on marking their contempt for Catholicism. In India, yet worse was sometimes visited upon local shrines or temples, for the native deities were largely regarded as pagan idols, and therefore fair game for what Burke described as 'the rapacious and licentious soldiery'.

Yet faith remained a part of daily life, and the experience of war sometimes brought men to a greater religiosity. George Robert

Gleig was the author of *The Subaltern; or, Sketches of the Peninsular War, during the campaigns of 1813–1814*, a justifiably famous, lightly fictionalized memoir in which he described his service in the Peninsula as a junior officer with the 85th Foot (later the 2nd Battalion, King's Shropshire Light Infantry). He took holy orders in 1820 (perhaps not surprisingly, for his father had been Bishop of Brechin), and went on to become first Chaplain to the Royal Hospital, Chelsea, and then, from 1844 to 1877, Chaplain-General to the Forces. He maintained his interest in the military, however, writing, besides an account of his service in America during the War of 1812, books about Wellington, Chelsea pensioners, and a study of military commanders.

In the event, it was not until more than a decade after the end of the Napoleonic Wars that clergy of other denominations were admitted to the Army Chaplains' Department, beginning with Presbyterians in 1827, followed by Roman Catholics in 1836 (after the Catholic Emancipation Act of 1829, in the passing of which Wellington, Prime Minister at the time, played an important part), Wesleyans in 1881, and the first Jewish chaplain in 1892. As it turned out, the admittance of clergy of other denominations greatly improved pastoral care in the army, and the numbers of chaplains increased markedly.

In 1816, a year after Napoleon's final defeat at Waterloo, chaplains were granted military ranks. The reason for the use of the word 'Department' as opposed to 'Corps' (the only 'department' in the British Army), was due to the fact that all chaplains were officers (as they remain to this day). It also ranks above any other administrative corps or department in the army for the reason that it has enjoyed the longest unbroken existence of any of them.

## MEDICINE AND TREATMENT IN THE BRITISH ARMY

In Waterloo's armies, medicine was basic, to say the least. Hygiene was poor, antibiotics non-existent and amputations – where one in three amputees died – were commonplace. If a soldier survived the battle but was wounded, the chances are he would die from an infection. If he survived an infection, the weakened individual stood a good chance of succumbing to disease. It has been estimated that in all theatres of war between 1793 and 1815, total British losses were in the region of 240,000 men, with probably less than 30,000 of these deaths being caused by wounds. As the table below shows, in Wellington's armies, disease was the biggest killer by far.

**Causes of death in British Army Hospitals, 1812–14**

|  | 1812 | 1813 | 1814 | Total |
|---|---|---|---|---|
| **Dysentery** | 2,340 | 1,629 | 748 | 4,717 |
| **Fever** | 2,235 | 1,802 | 409 | 4,446 |
| **Wounds** | 905 | 1,095 | 699 | 2,699 |
| **Typhus** | 999 | 971 | 307 | 2,277 |
| **Gangrene** | 35 | 446 | 122 | 603 |
| **Pneumonia** | 58 | 133 | 96 | 287 |
| **Tuberculosis** | 49 | 158 | 72 | 279 |
| **Diarrhoea** | 79 | 106 | 34 | 219 |
| **Fractures** | 6 | 64 | 70 | 140 |
| **Apoplexia** | 19 | 21 | 16 | 56 |
| **Tetanus** | 4 | 23 | 24 | 51 |
| **Hepatitis** | 5 | 23 | 8 | 36 |
| **Syphilis** | 19 | 11 | 5 | 35 |
| **Rheumatism** | 5 | 13 | 15 | 33 |
| **Epilepsy** | 3 | 6 | 2 | 11 |
| **Cholera** | 4 | - | - | 4 |

## Treating the wounded

Usually the injured had to be left on the field until after the battle was over and even then evacuation was slow. Many men spent days on the field surrounded by dead bodies and other wounded men, suffering from shock, thirst and the pain of their injuries. Local villagers would also descend upon the carnage to grab whatever valuables they could before military police drove them away. Many wounded men had their throats cut by the scavengers to stop them alerting patrols. Casualties unable to walk – even with help – had to endure rough passage on makeshift stretchers. They could be as basic as muskets or pikes slipped into the sleeves of greatcoats. Bandsmen, buglers and drummers were often the stretcher-bearers. In mountainous areas mules and donkeys were surefooted enough to carry men, and camels were used by the French in the Egyptian campaign. In Portugal, the use of unsprung carts drawn by a pair of bullocks could be noisy as well as agonizing; the solid wooden wheels revolved on ungreased axle-trees that screeched when they moved. The Portuguese believed that this sound scared away the devil. Leading surgeons of both the French and British armies tried to find ways of alleviating the suffering of wounded men by speeding up the evacuation process, and it was Frenchman Dominique Larrey who invented a flying ambulance (using a horse-drawn carriage) for getting men out of a raging battle to safety. Britain's Dr James McGrigor spent many hours trying to persuade the Duke of Wellington to improve medical evacuation, but with little success.

## Surgeons

Each battalion had one surgeon and two assistant-surgeons, whose competence varied greatly. If a soldier did suffer a wound on the battlefield and reach the hospital, his road to recovery was a long and dangerous one. Conditions in the hospitals were generally poor, and makeshift hospitals – often in commandeered cottages or inns – were overworked and inadequate. In the Peninsular War, the British Army lost 8,889 to enemy fire and

24,930 men to disease. The most sickly seasons were October and December, and disease tended to proliferate once a camp was struck and the men were confined in one place. When fever and dysentery took hold, as many as fifty men a day would die of disease. Hospitals and treatment stations were overcrowded, poorly ventilated and filthy. At Celorico in 1811, two patients per bed was normal. Sometimes they burned fir-log fires just to hide the stench of so many men in such cramped conditions.

Few soldiers had any idea of personal hygiene and no thought was given to sterilizing instruments, which often led to infection even from minor surgery. If they washed their hands it was only in a bowl full of water that soon became almost as filthy as the instruments themselves. There were no disinfectants and surgeon's smocks or aprons soon became filthy and germ-ridden. In the Peninsula, Dr James McGrigor did manage to establish small regimental hospitals that offered faster treatment and tried to make sure that larger hospitals were better run. This saved the lives of countless British soldiers who otherwise would have died from their wounds.

**Amputations**
Amputations were often the only real choice for soldiers who had suffered badly broken bones. During an amputation, officers were offered rum or brandy to mollify the pain, but enlisted men had to make do with a piece of wood to bite on. The surgeon's mates would hold the patient down, sometimes four to a man. The surgeon then tied a leather tourniquet about eight centimetres (three inches) above the place where the cutting would be done. A knife was used to slice down to the bone, with arteries pinned out of the way, before the surgeon began his work with the bone saw. There were two main types of saws used: a larger one for cutting through the thigh bone or femur, and a smaller one for the lesser leg bones and arms. Usually, if the amputee was lucky, the sawing would take less than a minute to complete. Next the arteries were sewn up and

linen bandages were applied, and then the stump was covered with a wool cap. It was deemed very bad form to utter a sound while the surgeon did his work, indeed Russian soldiers were actually banned from making any sounds either when wounded or being operated on.

Major James Napier was rather embarrassed when he swore for twenty minutes while the surgeon struggled to remove the limb with a blunted saw. At the end, the officer thanked the surgeon rather sheepishly. 'I must confess I did not bear the amputation of my arm as well as I ought to have done,' Napier later commented. 'I made noise enough when the knife cut through my skin and flesh. It is no joke, I assure you, but still it was a shame to say a word.'

Discarded limbs were often simply thrown out of the window, but on such occasions the results could be grimly comic. Lord Fitzroy Somerset, wounded by a musket ball which smashed his right elbow as he rode along next to Wellington at Waterloo, walked back to a cottage used as a field hospital to have his arm amputated. The Prince of Orange, lying wounded in the same room, told him that an operation had been performed, and the surgeon had tossed away the arm, which prompted Lord Fitzroy to call out, 'Hey, bring my arm back. There's a ring my wife gave me on the finger.'

### Wounds

For wounds where amputation was deemed unnecessary or impractical, the injuries were treated using a butterfly bandage, which was made of sticking plaster and bandage. It was first attached to one side of the wound and drawn tightly across to meet the other side, before being stuck together. A bandage would help keep everything in place and help the wound to heal. Stitches were made from cotton thread or sinew and were used to pull together larger wounds.

Bayonets, swords and knives left deep puncture wounds and were usually fatal if they were in the chest or abdomen as there was little the medical staff could do about them. To treat these wounds, surgeons often let the wound bleed for a while to clean it of dirt or clothing material, and in many cases actually increased the width of the injury to boost the exit of unwanted matter. About 60 per cent of wounds were caused by muskets, and even slight musket-ball wounds carried the deadly potential of infection as the projectile would take with it small pieces of uniform, as well as dirt. If bone had been struck then the resulting splinters added to the bacterial danger and there was always the risk of just bleeding to death. Deeply embedded musket balls – below the depth of a surgeon's finger – were regularly left inside the body and allowed to work themselves into a shallower position. Many veterans carried the leaden balls inside them for the rest of their lives.

## British Casualties (1793–1815)

|                  | Officers | Men    |
|------------------|----------|--------|
| Killed (total)   | 920      | 15,392 |
| Wounded (total)  | 4,685    | 65,393 |
| Total            | 5,605    | 80,785 |

## Walcheren 1809: a deadly fever

In July 1809 the largest British expeditionary force ever assembled sailed for the island of Walcheren in the Netherlands. Initial accounts described an area that was rather beautiful, a 'flat fen turned into a garden', but looks were deceiving. The water in the canals was dire and mosquitoes swarmed. Towards the end of the summer a fever took hold of many of the men and by early September there were over 8,000 cases in hospital. 'Walcheren fever' or 'Flushing sickness' was relentless. By November, the 9,000 troops stricken by sickness on Walcheren outnumbered those fit for duty.

Makeshift hospitals were set up in houses, churches and warehouses but conditions were appalling. The sick died almost by the minute and those waiting to be evacuated to Britain had to lie on the beaches in their own filth. By the time the expedition ended in February 1810, the fever had caused the deaths of sixty officers and 3,900 soldiers, compared with 100 killed in sporadic fighting. Six months later around 11,000 men were still registered sick.

In the subsequent Peninsular War, it was widely acknowledged that the Walcheren regiments were always the first to fall ill. Eyewitness accounts tend to indicate that Walcheren fever was a mixture of malaria, typhus, typhoid and dysentery. Higher mortality rates amongst troops compared to officers also indicate the poor state of most normal soldiers, debilitated by a life of poverty, campaigning and alcohol. Public outrage and a parliamentary inquiry blamed the army's medical arrangements, and the old army medical board was rapidly replaced by an improved 'new medical board'.

### The Malabar Itch

Wellington suffered a number of unfortunate illnesses, including bouts of dysentery, fever, lumbago and rheumatism, but perhaps one of the strangest and most unpleasant was the Malabar Itch, contracted in Bombay, which stopped him from going to the Red Sea to fight Napoleon's forces in Egypt. The Malabar Itch was a kind of ringworm accompanied by a fever and a blotchy rash. For treatment he had to undergo an unpleasant series of nitric acid baths which were so strong that the towels they used to dry him with would burn.

## List of stores for a hospital of 500 men in Wellington's army

| Item | Amount |
| --- | --- |
| Hospital tents and marquees, with poles | 2 |
| Palliasses (straw mattresses) | 500 |
| Blankets | 500 |
| Sheets | 500 pairs |
| Coverlids | 500 |
| Bolster cases | 500 |
| Rice | 2 cwt (224 pounds) |
| Oatmeal | 1 cwt (112 pounds) |
| Sago | 50 pounds |
| 45 gallon copper and trevet | 1 |
| Camp kettles | 50 |
| Pint pots | 200 |
| Quart pots | 100 |
| Trenchers | 200 |
| Spoons | 500 |
| Portable soup | 1 cwt (112 pounds) |
| Round tents, complete | 2 |
| Linen shirts | 200 |
| Nightcaps | 200 |
| Jar of oil with wick | 1 |
| Large tea kettle | 1 |
| Flesh fork and soup ladle | 1 |
| Scales and weights | 1 pair |
| Steelyard | 1 |
| Brass cocks | 2 |
| Spades | 2 |
| Shovels | 2 |
| Saws | 2 |
| Hatchets | 2 |
| Nails | 500 |
| Hammers | 2 |
| Knives and forks with carvers | 2 dozen |
| Vinegar | 10 gallons |
| Salt | 2 cwt (224 pounds) |

| | |
|---|---|
| Biers for wounded men | 60 |
| Flannel | 200 yards |
| Tea | 10 pounds |
| Sugar | 1 cwt (112 pounds) |
| Port wine | 1/4 cask |
| Bowls | 100 |
| Water buckets | 6 |
| Bedpans | 6 |
| Stool pans | 6 |
| Chamberpots | 200 |
| Basins | 10 |
| Urinals | 3 |
| Saucepans | 12 |
| Lamps | 10 |
| British spirit | 3 gallons and cask |
| Hard soap | 2 cwt (224 pounds) |
| Soft soap | 1 cwt (112 pounds) |
| Stationery and books | 1 box |
| Bathing tub | 1 |

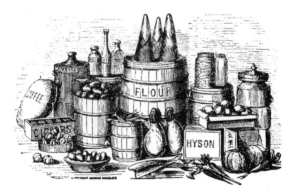

## WOMEN

Women always travelled with the British Army, but there were strict quotas for the troops, and in 1801 it was decided that six women were permitted per company with a maximum of two children. Often, however, the number of 'unofficials' numbered as many as 300 per regiment. Selection of those allowed to sail was carried out by drawing lots or throwing dice. 'To go' and 'Not to go' tickets were made and placed in a hat. Many of those wives who remained in Britain were left without adequate provision and so became destitute. Many more took to prostitution, a life which often ended in venereal disease and poverty.

In the Peninsula some 4,500 wives were 'legally' accompanying the army, not including the thousands of Portuguese and Spanish women who joined as camp-followers and prostitutes. Relegated to the baggage train, many of them rode along on donkeys. Most of the women were fiercely loyal to their men and to their regiment, and helped out with washing, cooking and nursing. It was said that they stuck to the army like bricks and when their men died they often married again – sometimes within days. Some had as many as five husbands during the war. Owing to the harsh conditions of life in the field, some women also gained a reputation as callous and cunning, with a liking for rum and foul language. After a battle they were often the first to scour the bodies for loved ones – and loot. Many carried sharp knives and would slit a Frenchman's throat before looking through his purse. Wellington was adamant that such women who indulged in such unlawful activity should be flogged, the same as any other criminal.

Conditions for the women on campaigns were just as harsh as those for the men, and sometimes they suffered more so. On the road from Corunna, Sergeant Anthony Hamilton wrote, 'Some of these unhappy creatures were taken in labour on the road, and amidst the storms of sleet and snow gave birth to infants, which, with their mothers, perished as soon as they had seen the light...'.

Officers were allowed to bring their wives, although, as in Wellington's case, they did not always choose to do so. Those officers who misbehaved with soldiers' wives were treated severely, because it was a breach of trust and demeaned their status. It was also considered a slight on the officer class to marry a woman of a lower social order. Keeping a mistress, on the other hand, was considered quite acceptable, and many officers set up these women in their own establishments, frequently acknowledging their children.

Wellington's marriage was strained and he maintained relations with many other women throughout his life. These included visits to brothels, mistresses and married ladies of his own class. There are 1,500 known letters to Mrs Arbuthnot, 842 to Miss Burdett-Coutts, 600 to Lady Wilton and 166 to Princess Lieven.

# TIMELINE:
# WELLINGTON AND BRITISH ARMY CAMPAIGNS

## 1769
The Hon. Arthur Wesley, son of the 1st Earl of Mornington, born in Dublin on 1 May.

## 1781
Wesley sent to Eton College.

## 1784
Wesley sent to military school in Angers, France.

## 1787
Wesley appointed to an ensign's commission in the 73rd Regiment of Foot.

## 1790
Wesley becomes MP for Trim in the Irish Parliament. Leads 33rd Regiment of Foot in combat in Flanders.

## 1794
**June** Duke of York's expedition to Holland. Arthur Wesley, aged twenty-five, embarks on his first campaign, leading three battalions at Antwerp to reinforce the Duke's standing against the Revolutionary armies. The Duke's position proves untenable, and the British armies fall back in retreat.

## 1795
**January** Britain withdraws from Europe after a disastrous campaign.

**March** Wesley leaves Holland and returns to London by boat. His Dutch experience was unpleasant, but it teaches him certain lessons, principally, 'what one ought *not* to do, and that is always interesting'. He also learns that many British generals did not really know how to manage an army or take a personal interest in the front. 'The real reason why I succeeded in my own campaign,' he writes later, 'is because I was always on the spot – I saw everything and did everything myself.'

## 1796
**January** Napoleon enters Milan. Colonel Wesley joins 33rd at Cape Town.

**5 October** Spain declares war on Britain.

## 1797
**17 February** Wesley goes ashore at Calcutta.

**17 October** Following Napoleon's triumphant campaign in Italy and the Tyrol, France and Austria sign the Treaty of Campo Formio, which agrees that Austria will occupy an area east of the River Adige, including Istria, Dalmatia and Venice, while ceding the Austrian Netherlands to France. A reconciliation between France and the Holy Roman Empire is to be discussed at a conference in Rastatt, Germany.

## 1798
**15 February** In central Italy the French-dominated Roman Republic is declared. Pope Pius VI shows his opposition, however, by refusing to relinquish his power, and he departs for Valence, France.

**March** The British victory over the Spanish navy off Cape St Vincent forces the resignation of Manuel de Godoy, the Spanish Prime Minister.

**May** On his brother Richard's elevation to the peerage as Marquess Wellesley of Norragh, Arthur Wesley adopts the original spelling of his family name, and becomes known as Arthur Wellesley.

**21 July** Napoleon secures Egypt when he defeats Mameluke forces at the Battle of the Pyramids.

**1 August** In the Battle of the Nile, a British fleet under Admiral Nelson destroys the French Toulon fleet in Aboukir Bay, Egypt, thus severing the French army's communication links with Europe, which establishes British naval domination in the Mediterranean.

**August** Wellesley sails to Madras with the 33rd to join in the campaign against the Tippu, Sultan of Mysore, a Muslim ruling over an overwhelmingly Hindu state. In overall command of the Madras army is Lieutenant-General George Harris; Wellesley is one of his deputies, along with Major-General Baird. The army numbers 20,000, of which 4,300 are Europeans.

**29 November** King Ferdinand IV of Naples declares war against France and occupies Rome.

**1799**

**9 January** The British prime minister, William Pitt the Younger, introduces income tax at a rate of 10 per cent on all annual incomes over £200 to finance the war against France.

**13 February** The Fourth Mysore war begins.

**5 April** Wellesley is ordered to secure the area of Sultanpetah village near to Seringapatam. The attack, conducted at night in a thick wood, ends in confusion and some loss of life, and proved a personal embarrassment for Wellesley.

**4 May** The British defeat Tippu, Sultan of Mysore, at Seringapatam. Colonel Wellesley, an acting deputy commander under Lieutenant-General Harris, is part of the British force. About 9,000 of the Tippu's soldiers are buried, while the British Army count 900 Europeans and 649 Indians killed, wounded and missing. The Sultan of Mysore is killed by a shot to the head. Tippu's kingdom is divided between Britain and its ally, the Nizam Ali of Hyderabad. Colonel Wellesley is made Governor of Seringapatam, a post he holds with some success for the next five years.

**1 June** Pitt the Younger finalizes the establishment of the Second Coalition of Britain, Russia, Austria, the Ottoman Empire, Portugal and Naples against France.

**25–27 September** General Andrea Masséna's French forces defeat a Russian army under Alexander Korsakov at Zurich. Field Marshal Count Alexander Vasilyevich Suvorov's main Russian force arrives too late, and has no option but to retreat across the Alps, while Austrian troops under the Archduke Charles withdraw to the River Danube.

### 1800

**17 January** The Treaty of Montlu appeases royalist hostility in the Vendue, western France, which allows troops to be released for a new French offensive in Europe.

**14 June** Napoleon defeats the Austrians at the Battle of Marengo, in north-west Italy, which guarantees the French recapture of Italy.

### 1801

**1 January** Under the Act of Union, the United Kingdom of Great Britain and Ireland is established.

**9 February** Following the successes of Napoleon's campaign in Austria and Italy, the Treaty of Luneville marks the virtual destruction of the Holy Roman Empire. New French territories also include Belgium and Luxembourg.

**21 March** France and Spain sign the Treaty of Aranjuez, which formally details their ultimatum to Portugal to break its traditional allegiance to Britain.

**2 April** Nelson defeats the Danish fleet in the Battle of Copenhagen, which was fought in response to Danish action against Britain with the closure of the River Elbe.

**6 June** The Treaty of Badajoz formally ends hostility between Spain and Portugal over the latter's traditional allegiance to Britain. Portugal cedes the province of Olivenza and consents to keep its ports closed to British ships.

**17 June** The confederation of Russia, Sweden, Denmark and Prussia (also known as the Armed Neutrality of the North) is dissolved when Britain, Russia and Prussia sign the Treaty of St Petersburg, which gives the British the right to search merchant vessels.

**15 July** Napoleon draws up a concordat with the papacy which effectively places the church in France under state control. Although the pope retains control of the Papal States, the French annex Ferrara, Bologna and Romagna.

**2 September** Napoleon fails in his attempt to capture more land in the east as French forces in Egypt led by General Jean Menou surrender to the British.

**1 October** Britain and France sign introductory peace agreements.

## 1802

**January** Arthur Wellesley leads a short expedition against a raja in Bullum, north-west of Seringapatam, which increases his experience of forest warfare.

**March** Wellesley's army of 9,000 marches into Mahratta Territory.

**27 March** France and Britain sign the Treaty of Amiens.

**20 April** On hearing that Poona was under threat from being set on fire, Wellesley embarks upon a forty-mile night march with 400 cavalry to prevent the feared attack.

**April** Arthur Wellesley is promoted to Major-General.

**23 October** At Poona, the maharaja Jaswant Rao Holkar of Indore is victorious in battle against Madhoji Rao Sindhia of Gwalior (the most powerful figure in central India) and Baji Rao (the peshwa of Poona and head of the Mahratta confederacy, who is sympathetic to the British).

## 1803

**30 April** The French sell Louisiana and New Orleans to the USA for a total sum of $27,267,622, which breaches the terms of the Treaty of San Ildefonso of 1 October 1800.

**3 August** British troops take the offensive against the Sindhia dynasty of Gwalior, which marks the start of the Second Anglo-Mahratta War.

**23 September** Wellesley faces the Mahratta Chief, Daulat Rao Sindhia, and his 40,000-strong army at the village of Assaye. Wellesley has just 7,000 troops, twenty-two cannon to Sindhia's one hundred, and his cavalry is outnumbered twenty to one. Although his guides advise him that there is no ford by which he might cross the local river, he discovers two villages facing each other across a bank and finds a ford nearby. Under fire from heavy cannon, his army crosses the river and a ferocious battle commences. Wellesley leads infantry charges against enemy guns, and captures ninety-eight of them, and has two horses shot under him (including Diomed, given to him four years earlier). General losses amount to 198 Europeans killed and 442 wounded, while the Indians suffer 258 dead and 695 wounded.

**Late September** Wellesley and his troops are victorious in another, less bloody, battle at Argaum.

**12–15 November** Wellesley leads the attack on Gawilghur, a fortress and town with approximately 20,000 inhabitants, and a difficult target. Its capture proves to be complicated, but in the end, Wellesley employs an escalade (climbing the walls with ladders) to good effect and is triumphant. The peace of Gawilghur convinces the Mahratta leaders of the futility of further resistance, and territory that yielded an annual revenue of £3 million, including Delhi, Agra, Broach and Ahmednuggur, later passes into British control.

**1804**
**21 March** The Civil Code is introduced in France, which provides a uniform civil law throughout the country.

**2 December** Napoleon crowns himself Emperor Napoleon I in Paris.

**1805**
**March** Wellesley, the 'Sepoy General', sails home to Britain, grateful for his chance to have gained experience in battle and administration. After suffering with numerous bouts of fever, lumbago and rheumatism, however, he was glad to be bound for home. He returns with a fortune of approximately £43,000.

**9 August** Austria joins an alliance with Britain, Russia and Sweden against France.

**21 October** Battle of Trafalgar, Spain; Nelson is mortally wounded and dies at sea.

**2 December** Napoleon crushes combined Austrian and Russian forces at the Battle of Austerlitz.

**15 December** Treaty of Schenbrunn is signed by France and Prussia.

**1806**
**15 February** French troops enter Naples, in southern Italy. Joseph Bonaparte, Napoleon's brother, becomes King of Naples the following month.

**14 October** Napoleon's forces defeat the Prussians led by Prince Hohenlohe at Jena, and the Saxons under the Duke of Brunswick at Auerstädt, both in Saxony.

**1807**
**8 February** Napoleon's army advances on the retreating Russian and Prussian forces at Eylau in eastern Prussia; in the indecisive battle that follows, there are heavy losses on both sides.

**7 July** The Treaty of Tilsit signals the cessation of war between France and Russia. Napoleon's victories against Austria, Russia and Prussia put him in an unassailable position in continental Europe.

**August** Arthur Wellesley takes charge of the division in an expedition to Copenhagen to seize the Danish fleet before the French capture it. Despite his lack of experience in European combat, on 29 August he leads his men into battle at Köge and beats the Danes soundly.

**6 September** Copenhagen surrenders. The whole campaign is a resounding success for the British – and a humiliation for the Danish. The booty accorded to the British is considerable.

General Wellesley returned to his position as Chief Secretary for Ireland.

**18 October** Napoleon sends his troops to Spain, where he replaces King Ferdinand VII on the Spanish throne with his brother, Joseph.

**19 November** French troops invade Portugal under General Junot.

**30 November** Marshal Murat's troops march into Lisbon, and the Portuguese royal family flees to exile in Brazil.

**1808**
**23 March** The French occupy Madrid.

**2 May** The Spanish cause an uprising in Madrid. Focusing on the French garrison, they stab or shoot at every French soldier they see.

**12 July** With instructions to drive General Junot out of Portugal, Wellesley sets sail for Corunna.

**14 July** Led by General Cuesta at Medina del Rio Seco, Spanish troops are defeated by French forces under Marshal Bessieres.

**22 July** Marshal Dupont is forced to surrender at Baylen.

**1 August** Under Wellesley's command a 13,000-strong British force lands at Mondego Bay, Portugal. Another 5,000 British troops, under General Sir Brent Spencer, sail from Cadiz. Wellesley is disappointed to discover that he has not been chosen to command the army. Sir Hew Dalrymple and Sir Henry Burrard, both in their fifties, are appointed instead.

**Mid-August** Wellesley engages in skirmishes with General Henri François, Comte de Delaborde, near Obidos and then, on 17 August, defeats the French general who stages a tactical retreat. The cost to the British is 500 casualties – almost four times that of the French.

**21 August** Wellesley defeats Junot at Vimiero. French troops advance using the Napoleonic tactic of the attacking column, which has been successful elsewhere, but they are destroyed by the controlled, rolling musketry of steady infantry in a line. Shrapnel is also used for the first time. In a bitter battle lasting two and a half hours, the French suffer almost 2,000 casualties compared to 700 British losses.

**22–30 August** In the Convention of Cintra, which provides for the evacuation of the French from Portugal, it is decided that the French will be transported home in British ships with all their stores and everything that they have acquired in Portugal, including much plunder. Wellesley, who is compelled to sign the treaty by Dalrymple, calls it 'an extraordinary paper'. The three generals are called back to England to face ridicule in the press, as well as the ordeal of an official Court of Inquiry.

**1 September** Sir John Moore is given command of the British forces in Portugal.

**30 October** The French evacuate Portugal and retreat to the line of the Ebro. Under the command of Napoleon's brother, King Joseph, the French army numbers 80,000. The Spanish armies total about 76,000 men, Moore has 20,000 and Sir David Baird brings another 8,000 reinforcements.

**8 November** Napoleon enters Spain with another 200,000 men, which causes the Spanish armies to scatter.

**13 November** Moore reaches Salamanca after marching a total of 320 miles at about eighteen miles a day.

**4 December** Napoleon occupies Madrid.

**10 December** Moore advances from Salamanca.

**21 December** British cavalry victory against the French under Marshal Soult at Sahagun.

**25 December** Moore is forced to begin his retreat to Corunna.

**1809**
**11 January** British forces arrive in Corunna. Anything that cannot be evacuated is destroyed, including 4,000 barrels of gunpowder, causing one of the world's largest and loudest explosions, which smashes almost every window in the city.

**16 January** Battle of Corunna. Moore is killed before he can evacuate to the waiting Royal Navy ships.

**2 February** Rome is occupied by a French force under General Sextius Miollis after Pope Pius VII refuses to recognize the Kingdom of Naples.

**28 February** Austria joins Napoleon's Continental System and supports the closure of European ports to Britain.

**19 March** Charles IV of Spain abdicates in favour of his son, Ferdinand.

**22 April** Wellesley returns to Portugal and takes command of the British/Portuguese Army.

**12 May** Wellesley defeats Soult at Oporto and forces the French to retreat. He achieves the victory after leading his troops in a secret crossing of the River Douro in wine barges and taking the French by surprise. In his astonishment Soult flees the town leaving guns and stores, bullion, sick soldiers – and his dinner, which General Wellesley and his staff eat instead.

**17 May** Napoleon annexes the Papal States.

**June–July** Wellesley becomes exasperated with the stubborn, old Spanish General Cuesta. After days of delay, the Spaniard finally decides to advance, by which time Wellesley can see the opportunity has been missed and declines to join him. Cuesta goes ahead anyway, encountering the entire French army near Toledo. He immediately retreats.

**5–6 July** Napoleon defeats the Austrian army under Archduke Charles in the Battle of Wagram, near Vienna, although the Austrian army retreats in good order.

**28 July** Wellesley defeats Joseph Bonaparte at Talavera. 'It was the hardest fought battle of modern times... Never was there such a Murderous Battle,' Wellesley writes later. He loses over 5,000 men, inflicting 7,000 casualties on the enemy. With dwindling provisions, and cursing his Spanish allies for lack of support, Wellesley is then forced to retreat in the face of advancing French forces.

**August** Wellesley's army sets up camp at Badajoz, but it is a difficult time for Wellesley, who has to keep his allies happy and his army united.

**4 September** Wellesley is made Baron Douro of Wellesley and Viscount Wellington of Talavera. 'Lord Wellington' is also made Captain-General by the Spanish.

**October** The secret construction of the lines of Torres Vedras is begun by Wellington's troops.

**1810**

**10 July** Marshal Andrea Masséna takes Ciudad Rodrigo.

**24 July** Craufurd is defeated by Marshal Michel Ney on the Coa.

**28 August** The fortress of Almeida falls to the French when they accidentally strike a gunpowder store hidden beneath the cathedral. About 500 allied defenders lose their lives, the artillery is wiped out and the British camp is devastated. Lieutenant-Colonel William Cox, the British commander of the garrison, urges his men to continue the fight, but he eventually surrenders.

**27 September** Wellington defeats Masséna at Bussaco. About 25,000 British and a similar number of Portuguese face 65,000 French troops. Masséna, despite superior numbers, cannot move the allies from the ridge, and loses 4,500 men in the failed attempt to do so. Wellington loses just 1,252 men, divided equally between the British and Portuguese. The battle – largely held to inflict maximum damage on the French – is therefore a success, despite Wellington's subsequent retreat towards his lines at Torres Vedras.

**10 October** Wellington enters the lines of Torres Vedras.

**14 October** Masséna discovers the lines, which block his route to Lisbon, and holds up his troops. On realizing how firmly Wellington has entrenched himself, Masséna is furious. Wellington employs caution, knowing that with supplies secured from the rear, he is in a superior position, while the French struggle with securing only limited supplies from the surrounding countryside. Thus begins a frustrating winter in which Wellington waits for reinforcements from Britain.

## 1811

**Early March** Masséna withdraws to Santarem with his army of 46,000 men, where he holds his ground, despite dwindling supplies. The French develop a cruel struggle for survival between the guerrillas who had allied with the peasants, and instigate ruthless policies of torture and execution to seek out food in the local countryside. The British – headed by the light infantry – follow them as they leave.

**5 March** Battle of Barossa is fought between Soult's troops and British forces from Cadiz under Sir Thomas Graham. During the clash Patrick Masterman of the 87th Regiment captures the first Imperial Eagle.

**10 March** Soult and his army take Badajoz.

**April** Led by Sir William Beresford, a mixed force of British and Portuguese troops lays siege to Badajoz, but without much success.

**10 April** Wellington issues a proclamation to the Portuguese people: 'The Portuguese nation are informed that the cruel enemy who had invaded Portugal, and had devastated their country, have been obliged to evacuate it... The inhabitants are therefore at liberty to return to their occupations.'

**3–5 May** Wellington defeats Masséna in a three-day battle at Fuentes de Oñoro involving nearly 80,000 troops. Wellington engages the retreating French army in a tough, brutal battle in which Craufurd's Light Division perform particularly well. Casualties are moderate – 1,522 British (including 259 Portuguese) and 2,192 French (including many officers).

**11 May** Almeida surrenders to Wellington but the garrison –
some 1,400 men – is allowed to escape as a consequence of
mistakes by Sir William Erskine, a British officer. Wellington
calls it 'the most disgraceful military event that has yet
occurred'. Lieutenant-Colonel Bevan, who is wrongly blamed
for the incident by Erskine, shoots himself to avoid a pending
court-martial.

**12 May** Beresford lifts the siege of Badajoz and retreats.

**16 May** Beresford defeats Soult at the siege of Albuera in one
of the hardest infantry contests of the entire period. Mortally
wounded, Lieutenant-Colonel William Inglis urges his men on
by shouting, 'Die hard, 57th, die hard.' Beresford loses 4,000
soldiers out of the 10,000 fighting, and Wellington comments
that a similar battle would ruin his army. Soult tells Napoleon,
'The British were completely beaten and the day was mine, but
they did not know it and would not run.'

**19 May** The second siege of Badajoz begins.

**17 June** After enduring numerous difficulties, such as officers
getting lost, scaling ladders being too short and having
antiquated brass cannon to contend with, along with the threat
of another large French army closing in, Wellington ends the
siege and orders the withdrawal across the Portuguese frontier.

**25 September** A short engagement at El Bodon takes place
between Wellington and Masséna's successor, Marshal
Marmont, the Duc de Raguse. Lacking support from General
Craufurd, Wellington withdraws to the Coa in Beira, tired but
glad that the French are no longer in Portugal. 'We have
certainly altered the nature of war in Spain,' he reports to the
Cabinet.

**Winter** Wellington remains with his army in Portugal.

## 1812

**8 January** Wellington embarks on his march towards Ciudad Rodrigo; as he and his troops get nearer, the men start digging trenches in front of it, as the siege preparations begin.

**19 January** Wellington takes Ciudad Rodrigo by storm, charging into an 'inferno of fire'. The attack is met with resistance and casualties are heavy, with over 1,000 killed or wounded. General Craufurd, his spine shattered in the assault, dies after five days of agony and is buried in the breaches of the wall. Despite the fatalities and injuries, Wellington declares the strike a success, having taken half the time he had anticipated. However he is disgusted by the behaviour of some of his troops who engage in drunken looting during the attack.

**February** Wellington begins the siege of Badajoz, organizing the digging of trenches, parallels, saps and mines, and the building of batteries and bulwarks.

**28 February** The Prince Regent bestows the title of Earl of Wellington upon Wellington.

**6 April** Wellington launches a night-time attack on Badajoz by force. Despite the long preparation, the assault is ordered too soon, costing many lives and causing many injuries. Troops advance on sharp spikes of caltrops and planks studded with upturned nails, mines, shells, grenades, fire-balls, powder barrels and *chevaux-de-frise*. The first and second stormings are driven back, and only after appalling losses do men of the 3rd and 5th Divisions eventually enter the town through the castle. British troops that survive the assault go on the rampage for three days and nights, breaking into houses and looting, raping women, stabbing children and killing men.

**Early June** The British Army march on Salamanca, causing the French to withdraw and leave behind strong garrisons in the town's forts. The French troops soon surrender.

**24 June** Napoleon begins his invasion of Russia.

**22 July** Wellington defeats Marmont at Salamanca. The 3rd Division make the decisive stroke in a short, fierce engagement. The French lose more than 13,000 men, twelve guns, two eagles and a number of standards.

**12 August** Wellington's allied army enters Madrid to a rapturous welcome.

**19 September** Wellington begins the siege of Burgos. After an ill-prepared attack on the fortress walls, the autumn rains flood the siege works. Transport and siege equipment are inadequate and ammunition supplies are low.

**10 October** Napoleon begins his retreat from Moscow.

**12 October** Wellington breaks off the siege of Burgos, deciding to leave 'this damned place'. His losses in dead and wounded are more than seven times greater than those of the enemy.

**22 October** The Allied army begins its retreat to Portugal, during which time there is widespread hunger, drunkenness, straggling and looting.

**19 November** The Allied army arrives at Ciudad Rodrigo to spend winter there while Wellington plans his next offensive against the French.

**1813**
**May** Wellington's army regains its strength and leaves for the Spanish frontier, marching from Portugal forever. Wellington turns in his saddle as he rides across the Spanish border and waves his hat, calling out, 'Farewell, Portugal! I shall never see you again.'

**21 June** With 80,000 troops Wellington defeats Joseph

Bonaparte's 60,000-strong army at Vitória. The French lose 5,000 men through death and injury, and 3,000 are taken prisoner; the allied casualties also number about 5,000, of whom 1,600 are Spanish and Portuguese. As the French are pursued back across Spain, they leave ammunition, treasures, private papers, prostitutes, animals and even King Joseph's chamber pot in their wake.

**28 June** Siege of San Sebastian begins.

**July** Troops under Sir Thomas Graham attack the French at dawn at San Sebastian, but by eleven o'clock Wellington is informed the assault has been unsuccessful, and heavy losses have been endured. In the meantime, Marshal Soult is gathering his army together to launch an attack on the allied centre and right.

**28–30 July** Soult tries to re-establish his forces in Spain, and comes close to succeeding, but at Sorauren, six miles from Pamplona, Wellington defeats him. Soult is forced to retreat into France.

**31 August** Graham and his men take San Sebastian by storm. The French are stoic in their resistance under General Louis Emanuel Rey, and 3,500 allied soldiers are lost in the battle. For the next three days, British troops plunder the city, with scenes of destruction as unpleasant as those witnessed at Badajoz. On the same day Wellington repulses Soult at San Marcial on the Bidassoa River.

**7 October** Wellington crosses the Bidassoa into France, establishing headquarters in St Jean de Luz.

**25 October** Pamplona surrenders.

**10 November** Wellington defeats Soult at the Battle of the Nivelle.

**9–12 December** Wellington defeats Soult at the Battle of the Nive.

**1814**
**27 February** Wellington defeats Soult at Orthes.

**Early March** Treaty of Chaumont is signed by Austria, Russia, Prussia and Britain, who all commit to fight against Napoleon in a united front.

**24 March** Soult enters Toulouse.

**30 March** The Russian–Prussian army enters Paris.

**6 April** Napoleon abdicates and is later exiled to Elba.

**10 April** Unaware of Napoleon's abdication, Wellington defeats Soult at Toulouse, with 49,000 men under his command and over fifty guns against 42,000 French troops, 100 guns and a good defensive position. The attack begins on Easter Sunday, and according to Wellington is 'a very severe affair'; the allies lose 4,568 men and the French lose 3,236.

**17 April** Soult surrenders, effectively ending the Peninsular War.

**30 April** Treaty of Paris is signed.

**4 May** Wellington is created Duke.

## 1815

**3 February** Wellington arrives in Vienna to meet Prince Metternich, the Minister of Foreign Affairs.

**26 February** Napoleon escapes from Elba.

**1 March** Napoleon steps on to French soil and begins the slow march to regain his Empire with a tiny force of about 1,000.

**4 March** Napoleon reaches Grenoble. He issues proclamations designed to stir his old troops: 'Soldiers, your general, called to the throne by the choice of the people, and raised on your shields, has come back to you. Come and join him! I am sprung from the Revolution. I am come to save the people from the slavery into which priests and nobles would plunge them.'

**6 March** Wellington meets with Metternich and other representatives of continental powers. The next day, he is informed of Napoleon's flight from Elba.

**20 March** Napoleon enters Paris and is greeted by delirious crowds as he drives up to the Tuileries at midnight. The Hundred Days starts. The Allies at Vienna renew the Treaty of Chaumont. Wellington is appointed to the supreme command of the Allied forces.

**Early April** Wellington arrives in Brussels to prepare for war with Napoleon.

**16 June** Wellington faces Marshal Ney at Quatre Bras, an area of farms and woods. Despite amassing his forces early in the day, the French general is inexplicably slow to start and the battle does not get under way until after midday. Fighting is fierce and the balance changes throughout the day. At the village of Ligny, troops led by Field Marshal Blücher come up against Napoleon's men, and are badly beaten. Blücher loses 16,000 men and is himself injured when his horse is killed under him.

At Quatre Bras Wellington has lost 4,800 men by nightfall.

**17 June** Napoleon's window of opportunity to attack Wellington's left flank diminishes as Wellington retreats north to Waterloo. Heavy rain in the afternoon turns the French pursuit into a muddy nightmare.

**18 June** After a miserable night of torrential rain, Wellington faces Napoleon for the first and last time – at Waterloo. Wellington has 67,000–68,000 men, a mixture of British, German, Dutch and Belgian soldiers, with 156 guns. Napoleon has at least 72,000 men and about 250 guns. But Wellington is occupying a favoured position – a ridge with a gentle slope running down towards the enemy, with shelter and concealment for the troops behind the crest – and Blücher's remaining troops are also marching towards the scene of battle to lend extra support. Napoleon's plan – to smash through the British lines up the road to Brussels – lacks subtlety. At 11.30 a.m. a single cannon fires three shots that start 'The Grand Battery' in which Napoleon pounds the British lines. On the left, a French diversionary attack creates a battle within a battle in the woods of Hougoumont that lasts all day. After half an hour's pounding, the four divisions of d'Erlon's corps advance on the British line. Napoleon hands control of the battle to Marshal Ney and the poor deployment of the French troops incurs massive losses from the solid British lines. One of the few British losses is Sir Thomas Picton, killed by a musket ball through his top hat. Impetuous charges of the two British heavy cavalry brigades complete the rout, but French lancers respond and inflict heavy losses on the British horsemen in turn.

By 2.00 p.m. the first of the Prussian troops arrive, slowly building throughout the day. In the afternoon, Ney launches a series of between twelve and sixteen cavalry charges. Unsupported by artillery or infantry, these are repelled by British infantry squares, each of which becomes 'a perfect hospital, being full of dead, dying and mutilated soldiers'. La Haye Sainte falls to d'Erlon's battalions – the only French success on the ridge. It is at this time that the British are closest to defeat, but the lines hold and by 5.00 p.m. the French cavalry is decimated. At 7.30 p.m. Napoleon launches six battalions of the formidable Imperial Guard, led by Marshal Ney and five generals (Friant, Cambrone, Christiani, Roguet and Harlet). The assault is seen off by British infantry lines and by Blücher's Prussians, who finally arrive to join in the defence. Wellington signals the battle has been won and returns to the inn where he is staying. That night he eats in his bedroom, with various members of staff in attendance. Towards the end of the meal he raises both his hands and says, 'The hand of Almighty God has been upon me this day.'

**22 June 1815** Napoleon is exiled to St Helena.

**5 May 1821** Napoleon dies on the island of St Helena.

**22 January 1828** Wellington becomes Prime Minister.

**15 December 1840** Napoleon's ashes are brought back to Paris and interred at Les Invalides.

**14 September 1852** Wellington dies at Walmer Castle, Deal at 7.00 p.m., aged eighty-three years and four months. A bracelet is found on his arm, which had been placed there by his wife when they were young.

## WELLINGTON'S APHORISMS

### On the Battle of Assaye
'All agree that the battle was the fiercest that has ever been seen in India. Our troops behaved admirably; the sepoys astonished me...'

### On the French commander Marshal Masséna
'When Masséna was opposed to me, I never slept comfortably.'

### On Indians
'I have not yet met with a Hindoo who had one good quality and the Mussulmans are worse than they are. Their meekness and mildness do not exist.'

### On surgeons
'I have served with all nations and I am convinced that there is nothing so intelligent, so valuable as that rank of man [the surgeon] in the English service... *if* you could get them sober, which is impossible.'

### On French marshals
Asked how he could account for having so consistently beaten the French marshals: 'Well, the fact is, their soldiers get them into scrapes, mine always got me out.'

### On Napoleon
'...unquestionably the greatest military genius that ever existed.'

'Bonaparte's whole life, civil, political and military was a fraud. There was not a transaction, great or small, in which lying and fraud were not introduced.'

'Field Marshal the Duke of Wellington presents his compliments to Her Majesty's Ministers. If they wish to know (his) opinion as a matter of public policy he must decline to give one. If, however, they wish only to consult him as a private individual (he) has no hesitation in saying that he does not care one twopenny damn what becomes of the ashes of Napoleon Bonaparte.'

'It is very true that I have said that I considered Napoleon's presence in the field equal to forty thousand men in the balance. This is a very loose way of talking; but the idea is a very different one from that of his presence at a battle being equal to a reinforcement of forty thousand men.'

## On Waterloo: before the battle

'There,' said the Duke, pointing at [a] red-coated English infantryman. 'It all depends on that article there whether we do the business or not. Give me enough of it, and I am sure.'

'I have got an infamous army (i.e. one of little fame), very weak and ill equipped, and a very inexperienced Staff. In my opinion they are doing nothing in England. They have not raised a man; and they have not called out the militia either in England or in Ireland.'

'Now, Bonaparte will see how a general of sepoys can defend a position.'

When leaving the Duchess of Richmond's Ball, on the eve of the Battle of Quatre Bras, Wellington commented: 'I don't like lying awake, it does no good. I make a point never to lie awake.'

## On Waterloo: during the battle

'Please, sir, any orders for Todd and Morrison,' asked a Cockney commercial traveller.

'No, but would you do me a service? Go to that officer [pointing], and tell him to refuse a flank,' replied Wellington.

When the 3rd Division asked to be temporarily relieved:
'Tell him what he asks is impossible. He and I and every Englishman on the field must die on the spot which we occupy.'
The Earl of Uxbridge was hit by one of the last cannon balls to be fired by a French gun at Waterloo. It flew into his right knee and shattered his leg. Turning to Wellington, who was sitting on his horse next to him, he said, 'By God, sir, I've lost my leg!' Wellington lowered his telescope for a moment to inspect the wound and said, 'By God, sir, so you have!'

**On Waterloo: after the battle**
'The hand of Almighty God has been upon me this day.'

'I don't know what it is to lose a battle; but, certainly nothing can be more painful than to gain one with the loss of so many friends.'

'I hope to God that I have fought my last battle. It is a bad thing to be always fighting.'

'I never took so much trouble about any Battle; & never was so near being beat. Our loss is immense particularly in that best of all Instruments, British Infantry. I never saw the Infantry behave so well.'

'Never did I see such a pounding match. Both were what the boxers called gluttons. Napoleon did not manoeuvre at all. He just moved forward in his old style, in columns, and was driven off in the old style. The only difference was that he mixed cavalry with his infantry and supported both with an enormous quality of artillery. I had the infantry for some time in squares and we had the French Cavalry walking about us as if they had been our own. I never saw the British infantry behave so well.'

### On Robert Craufurd

Craufurd of the Light Division was hit in the spine by a musket ball at Ciudad Rodrigo and took a week to die. In that time he apologized to Wellington for having been one of the 'croakers' who had complained to friends in England about Wellington. Wellington found the man overly sentimental. 'Craufurd talked to me as they do in a novel,' he said of him later.

### On victory

'What a glorious thing must be a victory, sir,' commented a woman of his acquaintance. 'The greatest tragedy in the world, Madam, except a defeat.'

'Nothing except a battle lost can be half so melancholy as a battle won.'

### On the Spanish

'They would fire a volley while the enemy was out of reach, and then all run away.'

'They were, no doubt, individually as brave as other men. I am sure they were vain enough of their bravery, but I never could get them to stand their ground.'

### On Nelson

Not long after his return from India in 1805, Arthur Wellesley encountered another man with whom he was not properly acquainted, while the two waited in a room in the Colonial Office in Downing Street. Years later Wellington recalled the meeting: 'I found, also waiting to see the Secretary of State, a gentleman, whom, from his likeness to his pictures and the loss of an arm, I immediately recognized as Lord Nelson. He could not know who I was, but he entered at once into conversation with me, if I can call it conversation, for it was almost all on his side and all about himself and, in reality, a style so vain and so silly as to surprise and almost disgust me. I suppose something that I happened to say may have made him guess that I was

*somebody* and he went out of the room for a moment, I have no doubt to ask the office-keeper who I was, for when he came back he was altogether a different man, both in manner and matter... All that I thought a charlatan style had vanished, and he talked of the state of the country and of the aspect and probabilities of affairs on the Continent with a good sense and a knowledge of subjects both at home and abroad... in fact, he talked like an officer and a statesman. The Secretary of State kept us long waiting and certainly for the last half or three-quarters of an hour, I don't know that I ever had a conversation that interested me more. Now, if the Secretary of State had been more punctual... I should have had the same impression of a light and trivial character that other people have had, but luckily I saw enough to be satisfied that he was really a very superior man; but certainly a more sudden or complete metamorphosis I never saw.'

It was the only time the two men – Britain's most famous sailor and soldier – ever met.

### On umbrellas
In 1813, Wellington saw several guards officers using umbrellas and sent this message to them: 'Lord Wellington does not approve of the use of umbrellas during the enemy's firing, and will not allow the gentlemen's sons to make themselves ridiculous in the eyes of the army...'

### On board
In April 1809, Sir Arthur Wellesley set sail for the Peninsula in heavy seas that soon turned into a gale, threatening to blow them on to the Isle of Wight. He was undressing when his aide-de-camp, Colin Campbell, dashed into his cabin to say that all was over with them.

'In that case,' Wellesley replied, 'I shall not take off my boots.'

## On Lisbon
'The most horrible place that ever was seen.'

## On his wife
In April 1806 Sir Arthur Wellesley departed for Ireland to marry Kitty Packenham, without much enthusiasm. 'She has grown ugly by Jove,' he whispered to his brother.

## On marriage
'How strange it is that two people can be together for half a lifetime and only understand one another at the end.'

## On writers
'If writers would adhere to the golden Rule for an Historian, *viz.* To write nothing which they did not know to be true, the Duke apprehends they would have nothing but little to tell.'

## On fame
'The Duke of Wellington has nothing to say to the forty or fifty Lives of Himself which are at present in the course of being written.'

## On his birthplace
Wellington was born in Merrion Street, Dublin, but did not consider himself an Irishman. 'Because a man is born in a stable that does not make him a horse,' he said.

## On education
'Be educated as if for the pulpit or the bar and then you will have a double chance of making a first-rate soldier. I would give more than I can mention that I had a university education.'

## On duty
'I am nimmukwallah... that is I have eaten of the King's salt, and, therefore, I conceive it my duty to serve and with unhesitating zeal and cheerfulness, when and wherever the King or his Government may think proper to employ me.'

## On women on campaign

'There shall be six women to every hundred men and these shall be drawn by lot before embarkation. All men shall have one pound of biscuits and one pound of meat every day, with wine if the meat is salt. The women shall be on half-rations and no wine, however salt the meat.'

## On his army

'It is quite impossible for me, or for any other man, to command a British Army under the existing system. We have in service the scum of the earth as common soldiers... The Officers of the lower ranks will not perform the duty... of keeping their soldiers in order... As to the NCOs... they are as bad as the men.'

After the Peninsula campaign: 'I could have done anything with that army. It was in such perfect order.'

'I will venture to say that in our latest campaigns, and especially when we crossed the Pyrenees, there never was an army in the world in better spirits, better order, or better discipline.'

## On desertion

'I don't mind the troops running away – they all do that at some time or other – as long as they come back.'

## On officers

'Really when I reflect upon the characters and attainments of some of the General Officers of the army... on whom I am to rely... against the French Generals... I tremble; and I only hope that when the enemy reads the list of their names he trembles as I do...'

## On nationality

'The national character of the three Kingdoms was strongly marked on my Army. I found the English regiments always in the best humour when we were well supplied with beef; the Irish when we were in the wine countries and the Scotch when the dollar for pay came in...'

## On the Peninsular War

In a despatch to Lord Liverpool, then Secretary of State:

'The French planned their campaigns just as you might make a splendid piece of harness; it looks very well until it gets broken and then you are done for. Now I make my campaigns of ropes. If anything went wrong, I tied a knot and went on.'

## On correspondence

'If I attempted to answer the mass of futile correspondence that surrounds me, I should be debarred from all serious business of campaigning...'

## On command

'I told [General Sir Brent Spencer] I did not know what the words "Second in Command" meant any more than third, fourth or fifth... that I alone commanded the army... and above all that I would not only take but insist upon the whole and undivided responsibility...'

## On the French

'We always have been, we are, and I hope that we always shall be detested in France.'

## On business

'My rule was always to do the business of the day in the day.'

## On mistakes

*Memorandum to his colonial secretary, William Huskisson:*

'There is no mistake; there has been no mistake, and there shall be no mistake.'

## On Ireland

We want discipline... the great object of our policy should be to endeavour to obliterate... the distinctions between Protestants and Catholics and... to avoid anything which can induce either sect to recollect or believe that its interests... are separate.'

## On Russia
'[The abdication of the Grand Duke Constantine from the Russian succession] will show that he agrees with others in thinking that assassination is the legitimate Charter of the Russian people.'

## On politicians
'The feeling I have for a decided party politician is rather that of contempt than any other. I am certain that his wishes and efforts for his party very frequently prevent him from doing what is best for his country.'

## On the Cabinet
'In truth the republic of the Cabinet is but little suited to any man of taste or of large views.'

## On Parliament
'After you have sat one or two sessions in parliament... you will probably be as astounded as I have been how England came by her greatness.'

## On General Alava
Wellington fought with General Alava at Waterloo and he told officials at Coutt's Bank: 'This is my friend and as long as I have money at your house, let him have it to any amount that he thinks proper to draw for.'

## On his own greatness
After a stranger helped Wellington across Hyde Park, he remarked gravely, 'My Lord, I have passed a long and not uneventful life, but never did I hope to reach the day when I might be of some assistance to the greatest man that ever lived.' Wellington replied, 'Don't be a damned fool.'

## On belief
A stranger approached Wellington and asked, 'Mr Jones, I believe?'

Wellington replied, 'If you believe that, you will believe anything.'

## On the offensive
When Stockdale the publisher tried to blackmail *Society* to keep names out of Harriette Wilson's memoirs, the Duke remarked, 'Publish and be damned.'

## On painting
When the artist, Sir William Allen, asked why Wellington was counting out banknotes instead of paying by cheque for his painting of Waterloo, Wellington replied: 'D'you think I am going to let Coutts's people know what a damned fool I have been?'

## On sparrows
To Queen Victoria, when she complained about the sparrow nuisance at the Great Exhibition: 'Try sparrow-hawks, Ma'am.'

## On music
At Vienna, Wellington was compelled to sit through a performance of Beethoven's *Battle of Victoria* (*Wellington's Victory*). After a Russian envoy asked him if the music had been anything like the real thing, he replied, 'By God, no. If it had been like that I'd have run away myself.'

## Napoleon on Wellington
When Soult advised Napoleon to summon reinforcements at Waterloo, the General reacted with some confidence. 'Just because you have been beaten by Wellington you regard him as a great general. I tell you that Wellington is a bad general, that the English are bad troops and that this battle will be a picnic... *Nous coucherons ce soir a Bruxelles*. [We will sleep tonight in Brussels.]'

## WELLINGTON: A PRIVATE MAN

Despite his public profile, Wellington remained throughout his life a largely secret and private man. 'I liked to walk alone,' he had once declared in India. He often left his house without telling his servants where he was going, and in war he provoked a certain amount of disquiet amongst his officers, who often wondered what he was planning. 'We hear little or nothing of Ld. Wellington, who keeps not only the Portuguese but the Officers of his Staff in the dark with regard to his Intentions,' wrote Lieutenant William Bragge of the 3rd Dragoon Guards in the Peninsular War. 'I understand at his own Table he rattles away to the General Officers etc., and fills them with Humbug Accounts which they have scarce time to repeat to their confidential Friends before an order arrives for the Brigades to march without Delay at least 20 Points of the Compass from the one expected.'

## WELLINGTON'S DISPATCHES

It was during his eight years in India that Wellington (then Wellesley) began writing detailed dispatches. By 1832, his correspondence covered 15,000 pages. However, Wellington was well known for the perfunctory, often downbeat tone of these dispatches, omitting mention of the actions of his officers or offering such faint praise that a victory might sound more like a defeat. Wellington simply could not bring himself to write a report in hyperbole and found praise difficult to bestow. Such oversights caused widespread dismay among those who served him and, towards the end of his life, he admitted he should have been more fulsome in his praise.

## BRITISH ARMY SLANG

**Abram:** to sham Abram was to pretend illness

**Bacon bolters:** Grenadiers

**Bad bargain:** a useless soldier

**Baggage:** women and children

**Bang up:** very fine

**Barker/barking iron:** a pistol

**Bat:** baggage, provisions, possessions

**Belch:** beer

**Belemite:** malingerer

**Bishop:** mixture of wine and water

**Bitch booby:** a country wench

**Black book:** regimental punishment book

**Blackguard:** a low person

**Black hole:** guardhouse or prison

**Blackjack:** half-pint tin mug

**Bleeders:** spurs

**Bloody back:** a soldier

**Blue plum:** a bullet

**Bog land:** Ireland

**Boots:** youngest officer in a mess

**Brimstone/brim:** a deserted woman

**Brown Bess:** British musket

**Brown George:** an army loaf or an unpowdered wig

**Buffs:** soldiers' belts

**Bulldog:** a pistol

**Bumbo:** brandy, water and sugar

**Bumper:** a full glass
**Butcher's Bill:** casualty list

**Cagg:** abstain from alcohol
**Calfskin:** a drum
**Calfskin fiddler:** a drummer
**Candlestick:** a bayonet
**Cap:** a shako, or military head-dress
**Caterpillar:** a soldier
**Clash pans:** cymbals
**Cool lady:** a woman who sells alcohol
**Cracker:** ammunition
**Crapaud:** a French soldier
**Croaker:** a moaner
**Crocus:** a surgeon

**Dead man:** an empty bottle

**Faggot:** man hired to appear for soldier at roster call
**Foot wobbler:** cavalry term for infantry

**Grog:** a mixture of rum and water

**Inexpressibles:** breeches

**Johnny Newcombe:** new recruit
**Jolly:** a marine
**Jonathan:** an American

**Knock-me-down:** strong ale

**Leg bail:** leave without pay debts
**Light bobs:** light infantry

**Muff cap:** a hussar's fur busby

**Necessaries:** personal kit
**Nightingale:** a soldier who cries out during a flogging

**Old trousers:** French *pas-de-charges* drum beat

**Parleyvous:** anything French
**Patlander:** an Irishman
**Piece:** a cannon
**Pigtail:** tobacco plug
**Poker:** a sword
**Pong:** bread
**Pop:** a pistol or pawning something
**Punk:** a female camp follower

**Rag carrier:** infantry ensign
**Rag fair:** inspection of underclothes and necessaries
**Rammer:** an arm
**Red rag:** British uniform's red coat
**Redshank:** a Highlander
**Roller:** neck cloth
**Ruffler:** a beggar
**Rumbo:** rum, sugar and water

**Saddle sick:** dislike of riding horses

**Saloop:** tea, milk and sugar

**Sheepskin fiddler:** a drummer

**Shifting ballast:** naval term for soldiers transported by sea

**Skilly:** thin soup

**Smabble:** kill in battle

**Smalls:** waistcoats, breeches, shirts

**Smart money:** compensation paid to those who lost limbs

**Snapper:** a pistol

**Snob:** a shoemaker

**Spit:** a sword

**Stick:** a pistol

**Stingo:** strong drink

**Stirrabout:** a stew

**Swad/swaddy:** a soldier

**Swizzle:** alcohol


**Tail:** a sword

**Tattoo:** drum call for evening

**Tilter:** a sword

**Time beater:** a drummer

**Toad eater:** an ingratiating subordinate

**Toasting iron:** a sword

**Tommy:** bread

**Trull:** a female camp follower


**Walking cornet:** cavalry description of an ensign

**Worn out:** a soldier unfit for active service

## NAPOLEON'S LOVERS

Josephine Beauharnais
Marie Louise of Austria
Marie Walewska
Desiree Clary
Pauline Foures
Mademoiselle Georges
Giuseppina Grassini

## NAPOLEON'S MEDICAL PROBLEMS

Colic
Peptic ulcers
Dysuria
Pituitary dysplasia
Oedema of the chest
Fevers
Constipation
Chronic gastroenteritis (when not constipated)
Prolapsed haemorrhoids (alleged)
Micropenis (alleged)

## NAPOLEON'S MARSHALS

Pierre Augereau (1757–1816)
Jean-Baptiste Bernadotte (1763–1844)
Louis Berthier (1753–1815)
Jean-Baptiste Bessieres (1768–1813)
Guillaume Brune (1763–1815)
Louis Davout (1770–1823)
Gouvion St Cyr (1764–1830)
Emmanuel Grouchy (1766–1847)
Jean-Baptiste Jourdan (1762–1833)

Francois Kellerman (1735–1820)
Jean Lannes (1769–1809)
François Lefebvre (1755–1820)
Jacques MacDonald (1765–1840)
Auguste Marmont (1774–1852)
Andre Masséna (1758–1817)
Bon Adrien Moncey (1754–1842)
Eduoard Mortier (1768–1835)
Joachim Murat (1767–1815)
Michel Ney (1769–1815)
Nicolas Oudinot (1767–1847)
Dominique Perignon (1754–1818)
Josef Poniatowski (1763–1813)
Jean-Mathieu Serurier (1742–1819)
Nicolas Soult (1769–1851)
Louis-Gabriel Suchet (1770–1826)
Claude Victor (1764–1841)

## HORSES: COPENHAGEN AND MARENGO

The Duke of Wellington's favourite horse, Copenhagen, was foaled from a mare brought back from Denmark after the successful capture of Copenhagen in September 1807. The horse was to accompany Wellington at Quatre Bras and Waterloo and, notwithstanding a hefty kick given to his owner on the night of his great victory, remained a firm favourite until long after the war. Wellington's close friend, Frances, Lady Shelley, rode the horse on more than one occasion, although found Copenhagen 'the most difficult to sit'. In Wellington's view, however: 'There may have been faster horses, no doubt many handsomer, but for bottom and endurance I never saw his fellow.'

Napoleon learned to ride a mule or a donkey in Corsica. He had a poor seat while riding and slid forward and back as he rode. In spite of this, he rode for pleasure as well as necessity and was considered both fast and fearless. He preferred smaller, good-natured Arabs with fair and patchy colourings, and had from ten to eighteen horses killed under him in battle during his career. His horses were thoroughly trained by a riding master, putting them through a series of battle tests that included firing guns, unsheathing swords, crossing bayonets, beating drums, waving flags and driving animals between their legs, all to teach the horses to remain steady in any situation. Although it is widely believed that Marengo was Napoleon's favourite horse, no horse of this name appears in the registers of Napoleon's stables or in any primary source. The horse named Marengo was allegedly captured during the Egyptian campaign, and legend has it that Napoleon rode it from the second Italian campaign through the retreat from Moscow, to the final battle at Waterloo. It was reputedly collected and taken to Britain, where it was put on exhibition. It is possible that Marengo was simply a nickname and the horse's real name was Ali, or Aly. Napoleon kept a number of horses and was fond of giving nicknames to each. Mon Cousin was nicknamed 'Wagram'; Intendant – 'Coco'; Cirus – 'Austerlitz'; Cordoue – 'Cuchillero'; Bonaparte – 'Numide'; Moscou – 'Tcherkes'; Ingenu – 'Wagram'; Marie – 'Zina'.

When Wellington's horse died in 1836, it was buried at Stratfield Saye in Hampshire. Asked later whether the horse's skeleton might be presented to the United Services Museum to complement the skeleton of Napoleon's favourite horse, Marengo, the Duke replied that he did not know exactly where the horse was buried. In fact, the Duke had seen the horse just before its burial and had flown into 'a most terrible passion' when he saw that one of the hoofs had been cut off. The mystery was not cleared up until many years later when a servant, who had taken the hoof as a memento, returned it to the second Duke, who made it into an inkstand. It has also been said that Mrs Arbuthnot and other ladies of Wellington's acquaintance had bracelets made of the horse's hair.

## WELLINGTON'S NICKNAMES

The Peer
The Beau
Arty (Arthur)
Nosey
Douro Douro (called by the Portuguese after his crossing of the
river at Oporto in 1809)
The Eagle (called by the Spaniards)

## VALUE OF OFFICERS IN MEN FOR EXCHANGE
## DURING THE PENINSULAR WAR

| Rank | Number of Men to Be Exchanged For |
|---|---|
| Captain-General, Field Marshal, General Commanding | 60 |
| General or General of Division | 40 |
| Major General or Inferior to Above | 20 |
| Brigadier-General, Colonel, or Adjutant General | 15 |
| Lieutenant-Colonel, Major, or Chief-of-Battalion | 8 |
| Captain | 6 |
| Lieutenant | 4 |
| Ensign | 3 |
| Non-Commissioned Officer down to Corporal, inclusive | 2 |

## FRENCH PROSTITUTES

With venereal diseases such as gonorrhoea and syphilis rife in his army, Napoleon introduced licensed brothels in the Grand Armée. The Napoleonic Code of 1810 enshrined the principle of forced medical inspections, and authorized prostitutes served the French army until the mid 1950s.

When King Joseph retreated from Vitória, he left behind him not only paintings and private papers, but also numerous women following the army and his court, described as 'un bordel ambulant'. August Schaumann reported, 'Most of these ladies were young and good-looking Spanish women, dressed in fancy hussar uniforms and mounted on pretty ponies... All they wanted was protection and a new lover, both of which they soon obtained, and they were to be had for the asking.'

## BRITISH NICKNAMES FOR THE FRENCH

| | | | |
|---|---|---|---|
| Beaux | Crapaud | Frogeaters | Frogs |
| Jack | Jacques | Johnny Crappo | |
| Mounseers | Parleyvous | | |

## DUELS

The preferred weapons for a duel were pistols, whose cased, matched pairs were part of the gentlemanly trousseau. Although it had always been an illegal activity, and punishable as attempted murder, injuries through pistol balls between gentlemen were always treated leniently. In 1798, a misunderstanding between Colonel Henry Ashton and Major John Picton led to a duel with tragic results. On 16 December they faced each other with pistols. Picton fired and missed. Ashton deliberately and disdainfully shot into the air. Within hours, Major Allen, another field officer in Ashton's regiment who had been slighted in the misunderstanding, challenged Ashton to another duel. Twice in one day a colonel accepted a duel against his subordinates – a unique event in the history of duelling. Allen fired first and Ashton was hit in the side. He remained standing and fired once more into the air. On hearing of the news, Arthur Wellesley rode all night to be with him, arriving two days later to see his friend for the last time. Shortly before he died, on 23 December, Ashton gave Wellesley his Arab horse, Diomed, which Wellesley was to ride until the Battle of Assaye, when the horse was spiked from under him.

In 1829, Wellington himself was involved in a duel with Lord Winchelsea, who launched a particularly vehement attack against Wellington, in which he accused him of popery for his concessions over the Catholic question. Winchelsea refused to apologize for his harsh words, and so Wellington called him out for a duel. They met at Battersea Fields on the morning of 21 March 1829. The event was brought to a swift conclusion, however, as Wellington aimed wide and Winchelsea raised his arm above his head and apologized.

## LOOT

At Seringapatam, the value of the treasures gained was estimated at £2 million, most of which was looted and only some of which was declared prize money for the army, the upshot being that most senior officers became rich. Troops often lost out in the distribution of money and goods, and payment of prize money could often take years to process. The truth was that a soldier was far more likely to get away with looting if he was of a higher rank. For them, such items were souvenirs or trophies. At Seringapatam the symbol of Mysorean power – the light green, silken standard with a red hand in its centre – was taken by Major-General Baird from the palace roof to Fort William. The gilded tiger's head from the Sultan's throne ended up in Windsor Castle. In complete contrast, if a common soldier was caught in possession of such items, he would likely face a punishment by flogging.

But it was not just valuable goods that the army might take. In the Peninsula, Wellington repeatedly issued orders to deter the men from stealing pigs:

> 'The Commander of the Forces requests the General officers commanding divisions will take measures to prevent the shameful and unmilitary practice of soldiers shooting pigs in the woods, so close to the camp and to the columns of march as that two dragoons were shot last night... The number of soldiers straggling from their regiments for no reason excepting to plunder, is a disgrace to the army, and affords a strong proof of the degree to which the discipline of the regiments is relaxed, and of the inattention of the commanding and other officers of regiments to their duty, and to the repeated orders of the army... The Commander of the Forces desires that notice may be given to the soldiers that he has this day ordered two men to be hanged who were caught in the fact of shooting pigs.'
>
> *Supplementary Dispatches and Memoranda of Field Marshal Arthur Duke of Wellington KG vi 588, vii 470*

During the sieges of Ciudad Rodrigo and Badajoz, widespread looting led to the towns being sacked, the savagery of which contributed to Wellington's later assessment that his soldiers were 'the scum of the earth'. Despite oaths from General Picton, calls from the trumpets and brute force from officers, who hit marauders over the head with the butt ends of broken muskets, the soldiers at Ciudad Rodrigo pillaged meat, loaves of bread, clothes and shoes. Worse was to come. At Badajoz, 10,000 British soldiers rampaged for three days and nights. Old men were shot, children bayoneted, women raped and churches looted. Most of the town's 21,000 population who had not fled were killed or wounded. When officers tried to intervene they were shot and only slowly did order return when a gallows was erected to hang those who were pillaging. A young officer of the 28th, Robert Blakeney, wrote: 'Every house presented a scene of plunder, debauchery and bloodshed, committed with wanton cruelty on the persons of the defenceless inhabitants by our soldiery; and in many instances I beheld the savages tear the rings from the ears of beautiful women who were their victims, and when the rings could not be immediately removed from their fingers with the hand, they tore them off with their teeth...' Sharpe was present at both sieges (in *Sharpe's Company*) and also at another episode ripe for plunder – Vitória – in *Sharpe's Honour*.

It wasn't until Vitória that Sharpe made his fortune, when hundreds of British soldiers poured into the city to plunder the treasure that the French had left behind, ransacking cases of Spanish dollars and trying on French generals' uniforms and ladies' dresses. Wellington commented, 'The soldiers of the Army have got among them about a million sterling in money, with the exception of about 100,000 dollars which were got for the military chest. The night of the Battle, instead of being passed in getting rest and food, to prepare them for pursuit the following day, was spent by the soldiers in looking for plunder. The consequence was that they were incapable of marching in pursuit of the Enemy, & we were totally knocked up... This is the consequence of the state of discipline of the British Army. We may gain the greatest Victories; but we shall do no good until we shall so far alter our system as to force the officers of the junior ranks to perform their duty, & shall have some mode of punishing them for neglect.' Although Wellington disapproved of such rowdiness, it is notable that Marshal Jourdan's baton and King Joseph's sword were both despatched in Wellington's name to the Prince Regent, who made Wellington a Field Marshal in return.

## Joseph's chamber pot

When King Joseph fled Vitória for the Spanish–French border after his defeat of June 1813, the King's coach was captured by

Captain Henry Wyndham of the 14th Light Dragoons. The coach contained a large number of rolled-up canvases looted from the palace of the Spanish king, as well as state papers, private letters – and Joseph's silver chamber pot. Captain Wyndham's regiment were dubbed 'the Chambermaids' after this event, and subsequently amalgamated into the King's Royal Hussars. 'The Emperor', as the pot is known, has since been used as a punch bowl, and forms the basis of a drinking ritual performed at the end of a guest night. The pot is filled with champagne, from which the commanding officer drinks a toast to 'the Emperor'. The Mess Sergeant Major then takes the pot to other members and guests who repeat the toast before handing the pot back to the commanding officer. It is his duty to select an officer to finish the champagne in the pot. If that officer cannot do so he is expected to tip what is left over his head.

### Wellington's favourite painting
Also among the haul from King Joseph's flight from Spain was Wellington's favourite painting. Correggio's *Agony in the Garden*, which now hangs in the Wellington Museum at Apsley House in London, is a devotional study of Christ in the garden of Gethsemane on the Mount of Olives, in one of the final nights before his crucifixion. The picture is a study in Christ's essential humanity and loneliness, featuring the moment just before dawn when his disciples sleep and an angel appears from heaven to give him strength. According to Benjamin West, the President of the Royal Academy, who valued the pictures at the time, it was one of two pictures (the other being by Julio Romano) that were so important they ought to be framed in diamonds.

### Tippu's tiger organ
Among of the Sultan of Mysore's collection of tiger-related treasures, he also possessed an organ, carved by a French craftsman, that depicts a prostrate European soldier being savaged by a tiger. When pulled, a handle in the flank of the beast caused the tiger's paw to maul the soldier's face, and reeds within the tiger's body made a snarling sound and a pathetic noise that

resembled the cries of the victim. On the fall of the sultan in Seringapatam, this tiger organ was taken from the Tippu's palace to Britain, and is now displayed in the Victoria and Albert Museum.


## MILITARY FIRSTS

### The Congreve rocket

Sir William Congreve, controller of the Woolwich Laboratory, was intrigued about reports coming back from India about rockets being fired on British troops by native troops. Congreve set about trying to create a similar force for the British Army and the Congreve rocket was the resulting innovation. Although Wellington was sceptical of its use, it did make further use of the shrapnel shell, an innovation made by Lieutenant (later General) Henry Shrapnel in 1784, but not adopted by the British Army until 1803. Sir William Congreve was also responsible for introduction of the block trail on artillery, in 1792, which lightened artillery carriages and improved their handling.


### Canned food

In 1810, François Appert, a Parisian confectioner, was given a 12,000-franc reward for discovering a way of preserving food for the army and navy. He found that food could be preserved against spoilage by first sealing it in an airtight glass jar, and then heating it. Appert's discovery was taken up in England by John Hall, founder of the famous Dartford Iron Works, and his associate Bryan Donkin in 1811. As well as using glass bottles, they developed the use of metal canisters made of tinned iron to store the food. Thus the world's first 'canned' food was made in a new factory set up in Bermondsey, south-east London. The cans were only used as emergency rations for the sick at first because they were so expensive; each of the early cans were handmade individually, from three pieces of tinned iron. The earliest cans were also quite heavy, and a hammer and chisel was needed to open them.

## The flying ambulance

Praised by Napoleon as 'the worthiest man I ever met', Dominique Larrey participated in twenty-five campaigns and over sixty battles and was regarded by many as the most outstanding surgeon of the Napoleonic era. He was a keen advocate of immediate amputation of a limb to avoid infection, and performed one of the first amputations at the hip in 1812. He is also one of the first to promote the therapeutic use of maggots. He created his 'flying ambulance' – a horse-drawn carriage used to evacuate the wounded from the battlefield – in the Italian campaigns of 1897, to reduce the critical time between injury and treatment. The flying ambulances were a success and served not only as a boost in morale but also created a greater and more realistic opportunity for the treatment and survival of the wounded.

## The Waterloo Medal

The Waterloo Medal was awarded to anyone who had taken part in one or more of the following battles: Ligny, 16 June; Quatre Bras, 16 June; Waterloo, 18 June. It was the first medal issued by the British Government to all soldiers present, and is also the first campaign medal awarded to the next-of-kin of men killed in action. It was also the first on which the recipient's name was impressed around the edge by machine.

## ARMY ENTERTAINMENT

### Hunting, shooting and fishing

Hunting was considered both good exercise and immense fun, and in the Peninsular War Wellington kept a pack of hounds which he named 'The Peers'. He often went hunting in the uniform of the Hatfield Hunt, a black cape and sky-blue coat given to him by Lady Salisbury. It was at such times that he was at his most genial and relaxed. 'Trigger clubs' formed for riflemen to go shooting game and, while marching to the river to bathe, the riflemen would extend into one long line and, backed by officers with hounds, startle game to provide the dogs with easy prey. Fish were abundant, and those soldiers who didn't bring tackle from home could catch the fish with smutted corn. Horse racing was also popular, which inevitably meant a wager on the winner; betting was always rife, and a number of jockey clubs sprang up.

### Dinner parties

In the evening, the regimental mess was usually open for dinner. The officers also enjoyed dinner parties, and Wellington was a generous host. A grand party was given to celebrate Lowry Cole's investiture with the Order of the Bath and Wellington lent his plate for the dinner which was followed by a dance attended by forty ladies and two hundred officers. Much wine was drunk, the band of the 52nd played throughout and, at about two o'clock in the morning, a number of Spanish officers offered to carry Wellington around the room. Declining, he suggested they should begin with the person of highest rank present, so the Spanish officers placed the Prince of Orange (Wellington's aide-de-camp) and General Sir John Ormsby Vandeleur in armchairs and hoisted them on to the shoulders of four bearers. The drunken bearers soon stumbled and fell, bringing down the Prince and the General with them. Characteristically, Wellington, who had ridden seventeen miles to attend the dinner, rode back to headquarters by 6.00 a.m. and was at work by midday.

## Sightseeing and shopping

When billeted in a town or city, British officers would visit many places of interest. After seeing every notable sight, it was the custom of some officers to visit the nunneries and convents. As with many foreign visitors, shopping – in local markets and bazaars – became an activity born out of necessity and curiosity. Others simply sought out the local brothels.

## Women and sex

British soldiers were forever engaged in the hunt to find women with whom they could speak and flirt. On Sunday evenings in some villages in Spain, everybody in the area would dress in their best clothes and come out to dance the scandalous fandango. The 'tertulia', on the other hand, was an open, informal reception held by local notables. Prostitutes followed the army wherever they went and local prostitutes could earn good money from the visiting troops.

## Theatre

Sometimes officers liked to try their hand at amateur theatrics, with performances in a make-shift theatre. In February 1813, Wellington and his staff rode over to Gallegos to watch a performance of Sheridan's *The Rivals*.

## Other activities

Smoking, drinking, writing letters, reading (newspapers, letters, books), horse racing, gambling, football (favoured by the Artillery and Highlanders), Fives (favoured by the Infantry and Light Dragoons) and 'Idle Clubs' (where officers smoked and chatted).

# APPENDIX

# BERNARD CORNWELL AND THE SHARPE NOVELS

## Bernard Cornwell (1944–)

Born in London in 1944, Bernard Cornwell was brought up in Essex. He eventually returned to London to attend university and, after a short period working as a teacher, he joined the BBC where he worked for the next ten years in television. He started as a researcher on *Nationwide*, a current affairs news programme, and later became the Head of Current Affairs for BBC television in Northern Ireland. When he met his American wife, he decided to leave his job at the BBC and move to the United States, where he worked as a writer. Inspired by Cecil Scott Forester's *Hornblower* series, which he had read as a teenager, he decided to write the adventures of a British soldier in the Napoleonic wars. *Sharpe's Eagle*, written in 1980 and published a year later, was the result. Spurred on by the success of his first novel, Cornwell then wrote a series of books that culminated in *Sharpe's Waterloo* (1990).

When the Sharpe series was televised in Britain, it created a whole new audience for the books, and Cornwell decided to continue writing about Richard Sharpe's military adventures. Although *Sharpe's Tiger* (1997) is the first book in the historical chronology, it was written sixteen years after *Sharpe's Eagle*.

Cornwell is a prolific author, producing two books per year, and in addition to the Sharpe series he has also written four books about the American Civil Wars (*The Starbuck Chronicles*), five thrillers that use sailing as a backdrop, three titles on the Arthurian Legends (that Cornwell rates as his best work), *Stonehenge*, *Redcoat* and *Gallow's Thief*, and a trilogy called *The Grail Quest*. Bernard now lives at Cape Cod in the United States where he enjoys writing and sailing.

## The Sharpe novels (in historical order)

*Sharpe's Tiger* (1997)
*Sharpe's Triumph* (1998)
*Sharpe's Fortress* (1999)
*Sharpe's Trafalgar* (2000)
*Sharpe's Prey* (2001)
*Sharpe's Rifles* (1988)
*Sharpe's Havoc* (2003)
*Sharpe's Eagle* (1981)
*Sharpe's Gold* (1981)
*Sharpe's Escape* (2004)
*Sharpe's Battle* (1995)
*Sharpe's Company* (1982)
*Sharpe's Sword* (1983)
*Sharpe's Enemy* (1984)
*Sharpe's Honour* (1985)
*Sharpe's Regiment* (1986)
*Sharpe's Siege* (1987)
*Sharpe's Revenge* (1989)
*Sharpe's Waterloo* (1990)
*Sharpe's Devil* (1992)

### Short stories
*Sharpe's Christmas* (2003)
*Sharpe's Skirmish* (2002)

# GLOSSARY

## SOME TERMS USED IN THE BRITISH ARMY IN RICHARD SHARPE'S TIME

**Adjutant:** Staff officer responsible for drill.

**Baker rifle:** Principal rifle used in the 95th Regiment. Created by Ezekiel Baker of Whitechapel, London.

**Bastion:** Defensive work on a fortress.

**Battalion:** Tactical infantry unit, comprising 500–1,000 men. British battalions usually divided into ten companies and were commanded by a lieutenant-colonel.

**Berm:** Narrow space or ledge in a fortification.

**Brigade:** Tactical formation of 3,000 men, containing two or three battalions. Until 1809 it was the largest formation in the British Army.

**Brigade Major:** Staff officer attached to infantry battalion.

***Brinjarris*:** Grain merchants contracted to supply the British Army in India.

**Brown Bess:** British smoothbore musket.

**Butt box:** Compartment, sometimes brass plated, in the butt of a gun for carrying rifle tools and cleaning kit.

***Cacadores*:** Portuguese light infantry or riflemen trained to skirmish.

**Caltrops:** Spikes laid on the ground to pierce the feet of cavalry horses.

**Carcase:** Incendiary of oil-soaked hay, fired from mortar or howitzer.

**Canister:** Artillery projectile of lead balls in a tin container that looked like a giant shotgun cartridge; also known as case-shot.

**Captain:** Officer, usually in command of a company (infantry) or troop (cavalry).

**Carronade:** Large-calibre, short-range cannon used on ships for firing canister.

***Chevaux de frise*:** Sword blades attached to a rotating length of timber, used by defending forces in a siege.

**Cock:** Lever in a musket raised ready to be released by the trigger that holds the flint. Setting the gun at 'half-cock' was a safety precaution because the gun would not fire; setting the gun at 'full-cock' meant the trigger would act and the gun would fire.

**Cobbing:** Corporal punishment used in the 95th Rifles involving beating the buttocks with a flat piece of wood.

**Colours:** Flags that represented the honour of a unit.

**Commissariat:** Agency of Treasury responsible for food, clothing, weapons and equipment in the field.

**Commission:** Warrant conferring authority, gained through purchase or outstanding performance.

**Company:** Basic infantry unit of 60–120 men, usually commanded by a captain.

**Corps:** Military formation (usually French) consisting of two or three divisions, commanded by a general.

*Compoo:* Indian term for a large contingent of troops.

**Counterguard:** Earthwork to protect base of curtain wall.

**Counterscarp:** Vertical face of ditch around fortification on attacker's side.

**Cushoon:** Circumcised Muslim soldier in Tippu Sultan's army.

**Cunette:** Trench along the middle of a dry ditch or moat serving as an obstacle to attackers in a siege.

**Curtain wall:** Main wall of a fortification, connecting two towers.

**Division:** Large military formation, commanded by a lieutenant-general, comprising approximately 4,000 men.

**Dragoon:** Type of cavalry.

**East India Company:** Incorporated by royal charter in 1600 to exploit trade with India and the Far East.

**Eagle:** French equivalent to British Colours.

**Eighteen manoeuvres:** Regulations setting out the movements in which all units had to be trained.

**Enfilade:** Term used to describe fire coming from flank.

**Ensign:** Junior officer, usually the first commission purchased.

**Escalade:** Attack on the walls of a fort using ladders.

**Exploring officers:** Soldiers who gathered intelligence behind enemy lines; also known as 'observing' officers.

**Facings:** Collars, cuffs and lapels of uniform jacket; colours varied between regiments.

**Fascines:** Long faggot or bundle of sticks used for filling trenches by attackers in a siege.

***Fausse-braie*:** Earth rampart used to protect base of curtain wall.

**Fencibles:** Militia-type units of battalion strength for home defence.

**First lieutenant:** Second-in-command of a warship.

**Flash in the pan:** Accidental charging of the powder in the musket pan that may or may not set off the gun.

**Forlorn hope:** Small group of soldiers who lead the storming party in a siege.

**Frizzen:** Hammer on a musket that is used to throw sparks to light the gunpowder in the pan.

**Gabion:** Cylinder of whicker or woven metal bands filled with earth, used to protect attackers in a siege.

**Galloper guns:** Six-pounder cannons drawn by horses in India to accompany cavalry.

**Glacis:** Gently sloping bank at the edge of the covered way of a fort to expose attackers to missiles etc.

**Grapeshot:** Close-range artillery ammunition; used mostly at sea.

**Grasshopper gun:** British three-pounder cannon.

**Grenadier company:** Elite company employed on right flank, composed of the biggest, strongest soldiers; title comes from when they used to carry grenades.

**Grommet wad:** Circle of rope rammed down gun barrel to stop shot rolling out when facing downhill.

**Halberd:** Sergeant's pike.

**Havildar:** Sergeant in an Indian infantry battalion.

**Holystone:** Block of sandstone used to scour decks.

**Horse Guards:** Buildings in Whitehall, London, used by the commander-in-chief of the British Army.

**Hot shot:** Round shot heated in a furnace used to fire ships or buildings.

**Howitzer:** Short-barrelled cannon for high-angle fire.

**Jemadar:** Indian officer equivalent to lieutenant.

**Jettis:** Indian strongmen employed as executioners by Tippu Sultan.

**Light company:** Elite company employed on left flank, composed of agile men and good marksmen.

**Militia:** Home defence force.

**Palanquin:** Royal carriage carried by slaves, used by Indian rulers.

**Parallel:** Trench dug by attackers to bring troops and siege guns closer to the fortress.

**Parapet:** Earth or masonry bank at front of trench.

**Paymaster:** Officer of captain rank responsible for regiment's pay.

*Picquet* **(or picket):** Infantry sentry.

**Pontoon bridge:** Bridge made of boats lashed together and covered in planks; Napoleon had his own *pontonniers.*

**Provost:** Forerunners of the military police.

**Puckalee:** Indian watercarrier.

**Quartermaster:** Officer responsible for supplies, rations, ammunitions, stores etc.; non-combatant.

**Ravelin:** Triangular outwork of fortifications, constructed beyond the main ditch and in front of the curtain.

**Retrenchment:** Defensive work by siege defenders to cut off breach.

**Revetting:** Shoring up sides of trenches.

**Roundshot:** Cannonball.

**Sabre:** Weapon carried by British cavalry.

**Sap:** Trench dug forward into a line to create a new parallel.

**Sapper:** Soldier trained in siege operations.

**Scrambling:** Slang term for deserting.

**Sergeant:** Non-commissioned officer ranking above colonel.

**Sergeant-Major:** Senior sergeant in battalion.

**Shako:** Peaked, cylindrical hat usually made of felt.

**Shell:** Artillery ammunition.

*Silladars*: Mercenary Indian horsemen.

**Sortie:** Attack by besieged defenders outside their own defence.

**Sponger:** Artillery man charged with cleaning out the barrel.

**Stock:** Uncomfortable leather collar worn around the neck by British troops.

**Subadar:** Indian infantry rank equivalent to captain.

**Subaltern:** Junior officer of ensign.

**Sub-unit:** British term referring to company, platoon or troop of men.

**Terre plein:** Flat surface behind rampart, usually with parapet, on which defenders place cannons.

**Town major:** Staff officer permanently posted to specific town, responsible for military administration.

***Tulwar:*** Curved Indian sword.

**Windage:** The difference between the calibre of ball and bore of barrel.

# BIBLIOGRAPHY AND SOURCES

## Books

MARK ADKIN, *The Sharpe Companion: A historical and military guide to Bernard Cornwell's Sharpe novels 1777–1808 Volume I: The Early Years* (London, HarperCollins, 2003)

MARK ADKIN, *The Sharpe Companion: A detailed historical and military guide to Bernard Cornwell's bestselling series of Sharpe novels* (London, HarperCollins, 2000)

B. J. BLUTH, *Marching with Sharpe* (London, HarperCollins, 2001)

PHILIP GUEDALLA, *The Duke* (London, 1931)

CHRISTOPHER HIBBERT, *Wellington: A Personal History* (London, HarperCollins, 1997)

NICHOLAS HOBBES, *Essential Militaria* (London, Atlantic Books, 2003)

RICHARD HOLMES, *Redcoat: The British Soldier in the Age of Horse and Musket* (London, HarperCollins, 2001)

Edited and with a foreword by CAPTAIN B. H. LIDDEL HART, *The Letters of Private Wheeler, 1809–1828* (Michael Joseph, 1951)

MARK URBAN, *Rifles: Six Years with Wellington's Legendary Sharpshooters* (London, Faber, 2003)

Edited and arranged by JUXON BARTON, *The Duke of Wellington, What they said and what he said,* (Kettering, J. L. Carr)

These are good books and excellent sources of information about Wellington and his armies in the period covered by the Sharpe novels. Those novels are listed in the Appendix; they are published by HarperCollins in the UK, and by Penguin in the USA.

## Websites

Besides the many books about Wellington and his army of the time, and ancillary subjects, there are a great many websites that deal, in part or in whole, with the subject. Below are some of the best:

**www.angelfire.com/wy/dukeofwellington**

**www.napoleon.org**

**www.napoleonguide.com**

**www.bernardcornwell.net**

**www.sharpetorium.info**

**www.wtj.com/wars/napoleonic**

**www.napoleon-series.org**

**www.regiments.org**

**www.militaryheritage.com**

**www.wargames.co.uk**

## Museums and places to visit

Finally, mention must be made of some of the places that can be visited around the country in connection with Wellington, his life and achievements. Apsley House, now the Wellington Museum, on Hyde Park Corner in London contains an impressive collection of Wellington's trophies and paintings, including the sword that he wore at the Battle of Waterloo and his favourite painting, Correggio's *Agony in the Garden*. An equally good place to visit in London is the Guards Museum, next to Wellington Barracks, which explores the history of the Guards regiment in the army. Stratfield Saye House, in Hampshire, was given to Wellington by the British Government for his victory at the Battle of Waterloo. Walmer Castle, in Kent, was his residence as Lord Warden of the Cinque Ports, and was also the site of his death. Wellington is buried in St Paul's Cathedral.

# INDEX

* In the lists of battle honours
(see examples on page 49)
the British Army used the
spellings marked with an
asterisk. These spellings were
also used on a regiment's
colours when details of
specific battle honours were
selected for special mention.